Letting Go In Love

Letting Go In Love

Reflections on Spiritual Formation

Foreword by Cardinal Hume

JOHN DALRYMPLE

Michael Glazier
Wilmington, DE

First published in 1988 by Michael Glazier, Inc., 1935 West Fourth Street, Wilmington, Delaware, 19805 in cooperation with Darton, Longman and Todd, Ltd, 89 Lillie Road, London SW6 1UD. This collection and chapters 1, 4, 5, 9, 10, 11, 12 ©1986, Charles Barclay. Chapters 2, 6, and 8 ©1986, the Estate of John Dalrymple. Chapter 3 ©1985, *The Way*. Chapter 7 ©1985, *The Clergy Review*. Library of Congress Catalog Card Number: 87-45005. International Standard Book Number: 0-89453-618-4. Typography: Input Typesetting Ltd, London SW19 8 DR. Printed in the United States of America.

Contents

Foreword

This volume reveals the development over the last decade of the inner life and thought of Father John Dalrymple. His own natural reticence is gently countered in an introductory section written by two priests who were close friends. Their personal contributions help the reader to see behind the scenes into a life-style which inspired and challenged so many people to live the Gospel. Father Jock never pretended this was an easy way of life, but insisted again and again that prayer was the essential way of reaching out to God, and he demonstrated that contemplative prayer was available to all. Unless we base our lives on prayer we cannot be more than superficial followers of Jesus Christ.

In his essays we read how Father Dalrymple always desired union with God and thought initially that this required him to be impassive or slightly detached from the struggles of the world. But over the years his attitude changed as he matured spiritually. In his final essay on spiritual formation he says with profound simplicity that the more sensitive we are to God, the nearer we are likely to be to God's view, to the mind of Christ.

His own personal growth mirrored a similar awareness in the Church in recent years, both at local and international levels. There is a new understanding of community as important to Christian living. We can never be content with saving our own souls in isolation. We have to be concerned too for the people of other nations, and especially those most in need. For this reason he supported one of his assistant priests who went to work in Latin America and kept up a lively correspondence with him. It is not without significance that Father Jock's last days were spent visiting that priest, who was recovering from an illness contracted in Central America.

BASIL HUME
Archbishop of Westminster

Acknowledgements

Chapter 2 was previously published by the Catholic Truth Society (1985), chapter 3 in *The Way* (1985), chapter 6 in *Mount Carmel* (1968), chapter 7 in *The Clergy Review* (1985), chapter 8 in *Beda Review* (1984). Chapter 5 is based on a paper given to the Glasgow Circle of the Newman Association (1985) and chapter 12 on an address given to the Dunkeld Diocesan Congress at Dundee (1985). 'Walking Away' from *The Gate* by C. Day Lewis is quoted by permission of the Executors of the Estate of C. Day Lewis and Jonathan Cape, Ltd.

Many thanks to Eileen A. Millar for her editorial work on this volume.

Biographical Introduction

Sunday, 8 April 1928 was Easter Sunday. As was their custom, Sir Hew Hamilton Dalrymple and his wife Nancie came to Mass at eleven o'clock. Lady Dalrymple played the organ for the great feast of the resurrection. At six o'clock that same evening she gave birth to a boy child. He was baptized with the names John David. His father used to call him, as the youngest child, 'my Paschal Benjamin'.

One of four children, John (immediately and lastingly called Jock) grew up happily in his family, was sent away to a prep school (Avisford in Sussex), and subsequently to Ampleforth, the well known and successful Benedictine school ·some thirty miles from York.

A great influence in Jock's school life was Father Stephen Marweed, an unsung saint, a simple, silent, powerful monk of Ampleforth who loved the Lord so deeply that his goodness literally infected Jock and many others who came near him. And there is no doubt that a foundational and permeating strength for Jock was the remarkable spiritual depth, commitment and daily living of his father and mother. Outwardly they were 'landed gentry' living the life of East Lothian and Scotland which was expected from their position. Hidden beneath that was the daily routine of lengthy periods of deep prayer, Mass and generous unknown work with the poor and deprived.

Like so many of his generation, Jock was swept up into compulsory military service. He was not naturally a soldier, but there is no doubt his two years with the Scots Guards, serving in London, gave him a discipline and dimension which remained with him and coloured the rest of his life. It also sowed for him lasting personal links which were richly valuable in his subsequent pastoral work. Some of these were secular friendships which gave him an entry to a wide range of non-Catholic relationships as a priest. He also gained a particular insight from his contact and closeness to Canon Alfonso de Zulueta in Chelsea, a man of intellect, humility and deep spirituality, combined with a breadth of pastoral awareness and practice which covered the wide social spectrum of his Chelsea parish and beyond.

Another formative contact was Monsignor Vernon Johnson. Jock's father had long been a devotee of St Thérèse of Lisieux. Vernon Johnson had literally come into the Roman Catholic Church as a result of reading her autobiography. The influence of her spirituality is very evident in the writings and life style of Jock's priestly years. Indeed, had he not died so suddenly and unexpectedly in Florida, his plan had been to come back to Scotland and then make a pilgrimage to Lisieux to pray out his new future under her guidance. Jock also came to love the life and message of Charles de Foucauld. De Foucauld's spirit and example strengthened and salted Jock's own spiritual journey, even leading him on pilgrimage as a priest to Charles's hermitage at Tamanrasset in the Sahara.

For priestly training, Jock was sent to the Scots College in Rome. These years were invaluable not only for the philosophical and theological foundation which they gave him, but also for the day-by-day contact with and friend-ship of many students from very different Scottish back-grounds outside his experience. These lasting relationships opened doors in the length and breadth of Scotland. Future priests knew Jock as a man of prayer, an intelligent and thoughtful person, a shy yet open friend, a humorous and entertaining companion.

After ordination in Rome in 1954, Jock was rapidly sent as a lecturer to the new diocesan seminary for St Andrews and Edinburgh at Drygrange on the borders. But a year later he was given an opportunity for direct, local pastoral work – the work longed for by any newly ordained priest. He had three years at St Mary's Cathedral, in the centre of Edinburgh. This was a time he deeply loved. He penetrated areas of deprivation and need which led to his personal vision and founding of Martin House. This was a project for the accommodation and eventual rehabilitation of any women in need. Such need was wide-ranging. There were women who had simply fallen on bad times, had no home and no work; there were some who were mentally unstable or disorientated; there were prostitutes and ex-prostitutes. Over the years, with able help and care from lay workers, Martin House was a haven of refuge for many in need. Jock and his co-workers have long been ready to meet the Lord who is quoted in the gospel of Matthew, chapter 25.

From staying there with him, I know that he had already adopted two planks of his way of life which remained with him for the rest of his days, but were not broadcast to the generality of people. The first was that he normally slept on the floor, as an act of humility and penance. Even after his severe heart attacks, he was determined to continue this practice. For him it was an important personal expression of an aceticism which did not have to be public, but was a night-by-night reference to his desire to give himself totally to his Lord and his people.

The second plank – which we spoke of often and agreed as a foundation for spiritual growth and pastoral effectiveness – was early rising and a prolonged period of personal prayer each day, normally before the rest of the local household had surfaced. This scheduled appointment with God reminds me of the psalm:

I rise before dawn and cry for help,
I hope in your word.
My eyes watch through the night
to ponder your promise. (Ps. 119:147–8)

In 1960, Jock was posted back to Drygrange as spiritual director. He spent ten years there, the years which were turbulent in most student communities. There was an upsurge of interest and action about justice, peace, banning the bomb, student rights and so on. It was also the period of the first thrills of Vatican II with its opening of windows, liturgical redevelopment and wide-ranging discussion of all manner of theological and ecclesiastical matters.

The leader of the seminary, Mgr Barry, gave every support to Jock and his approach to the spiritual growth of the students. In return, Jock was a great moral and spiritual source for Mgr Barry and other members of the staff. This was a period of personal spiritual development, theological inquiry and a rich experience of guidance and counselling, both within the seminary situation, and in the gradually increasing contacts made from talks, retreats and correspondence beyond the Drygrange circle.

In one of our long discussions together when Jock was feeling somewhat depressed and was wondering about his effectiveness for the students, his mission in the life of the Church and how he could do more for God, I urged him strongly and seriously to branch out into writing. Jock was shy of doing this. He felt that he could not write and that he had nothing to say. It may seem strange that one so gifted in expressing the depth of communion with God, insights into theological understanding and personal counselling was nevertheless quite unaware of the potential which he had for furthering an apostolate of the love of God for many people all over the world. The production of this book is in itself a testimony to Jock's gift of communicating not only in the spoken but also in the written word.

So it was that from 1970 onwards there was a continuous flow of articles and books from Jock's pen. The depth of his penetration and the width of his appeal were not measured in his lifetime, but it is enough to say that an article which is reproduced in this volume had a postscript from the editors of *The Way* which reads as follows:

> John Dalrymple completed this article shortly before his sudden death in the United States in September 1985. Without doubt he was one of the most able and stimulating writers on spirituality in the United Kingdom. We would like to record our gratitude for his contributions to *The Way/Way Supplements* over the years.

I have no doubt that this book and much of his already published material will continue to be an inspiration to people young and old, in lay situations and in the religious life – especially perhaps those who are members of the stricter and more enclosed orders.

I think it will always be hard to establish just how wide was the influence which Jock exerted. Much of it was very deeply personal and unlikely ever to be made public. But the reaction to his death has been a shoal of letters to his family. Some have come from friends and relations who are known, but the greater majority are from hitherto totally unknown people around the world, members of religious orders, married and single, male and female, old, middling and young, black and white, highly educated and almost illiterate, and across the whole spectrum of religious denomination, non-Christian belief and atheism or agnosticism.

In 1970 Jock was quite unexpectedly moved by his bishop to take up duty as chaplain to the students at St Andrews University. Already completely involved with young men in the seminary who were of the student age-range, Jock was nevertheless faced with a twofold challenge. In the first place the students were both male and female; they were also not committed to God in the same way as the seminarians. Both with the staff and the university students, Jock encountered a broader and tougher challenge to his own faith and to the translation of that faith to sceptical, lapsing, agnostic or even atheistic young people.

Secondly, for the first time in his life, Jock found himself master of his own household, responsible for day-by-day living conditions, organizing of a routine and timetable, buyer of provisions, banker of monies, payer of bills, cleaner of loos, repairer of drainpipes, conserver of cash, both petty and bulk. His initial reaction was close to panic, but his utter faith in God, his acceptance of the present moment and his reliance upon St Thérèse of Lisieux's 'little way' opened him in a new dimension. He found the students difficult at the beginning, but he soon came to terms with the openness and need for irregular life-style which is peculiar to student existence. Once he had accepted this and adjusted, he laid the foundation for his future approach to the ordinary parish apostolate . . . what I have come, over a long time, to call 'the open house'.

While he was both learning and giving in the university setting, Jock was also benefiting from the different tempo of life and contacts. To be at Drygrange and subsequently at St Andrews meant that there were definite vacation periods. These he came to fill more and more with retreats and outside engagements for talking, for leading prayer, for ecumenical dialogue. The last, perhaps as much as anything, was vital for Jock and for the Church. Passionately Scottish, passionately Catholic, Jock was also passionately ecumenical. He really cared about Christ's call that 'they may all be one'. And for this he worked in every possible way. No doubt this deep inner desire and his own personality led to his appointment as the first Catholic observer to attend the Assembly of the Church of Scotland in 1969.

I suppose that those who came spiritually into relationship with Jock in a special way were any individuals or groups who could come collectively under the title of 'contemplative'. To me personally it was a thing of wonder and encouragement – when invited now and then to give a retreat to a Carmelite monastery, a group of diocesan priests in Ireland or England, an ecumenical gathering on prayer and so on – to find that Jock had been there the year before and that the memory of his visit and his teaching was freshly green in their lives. Moreover many had received follow-up letters of support, elucidation or guidance written by him in a prayerful assurance of God's love and care.

Jock's writing developed steadily in depth, clarity and insight. Through the combination of prayer and theological study he was able to express in his articles and books the profound truths of God in readily available language, with frequent turns of phrase which lit up previously obscure points and planted them in the reader's memory. Later in his life these areas of knowledge and experience were further enriched by his living priesthood in the parochial setting of St Ninian's, Marionville, Edinburgh, by his increasing interest in and care for the peoples of the developing world, and by his own intimate encounter with dying before death as he suffered a couple of severe heart attacks.

Anyone who followed the parochial life of St Ninian's in the ten years 1975–85 will have been aware of the implementation of Vatican II. Jock opened up the house gradually, welcomed the poor and homeless as well as the ordinary parishioners. He moved towards a parochial council which was so well established by the time he suffered his heart attacks that the parishioners were able to cope with the continuance of all aspects of the parish except the strictly priestly functions. In facing the development of the liturgy, Jock literally turned the church building of St Ninian's back to front – an excellent and worshipful decision. In his whole approach and sensitivity to the reaction of the local people, Jock became a prophet in his own country. The way he lived and the vision he had of the life of local community was a challenge, perhaps even a threat, to some fellow priests.

One of the growth areas was in opening up concern for justice and peace, especially in relation to the Third World or developing countries. Jock preached in Kenya and Uganda, in Israel and the USA. Latterly he became interested in South and Central America. Parochially, it is not always easy to lift the concerns of local need beyond parish boundaries and into the crying needs of the 'have-nots'. It is an interesting phenomenon that the effort to involve ordinary people in concerns beyond their own narrow boundaries does not in fact reduce effective action at home, but rather produces extra energy and generosity which flows to both local and international need.

When he came through his severe heart attacks, I was privileged to spend some time with him at the family home at Leuchie, North Berwick. Jock had been to the threshold of death. Coming back from the brink, he had to face a

radical readjustment to his way of life. Walking, talking
and praying together around the home grounds and across
the golf course, he came to terms with God's action in his
life, accepted need for greater care of himself, but insisted
on retaining much of his ascetic way of life. Though few
would have known it, Jock was moving more and more
towards a life of ascetic poverty and freedom from administration. For a considerable time, he considered moving
from parochial life to a lay community, but eventually we
agreed that his health would not stand that particular way
of life. Resignedly and peacefully, he continued with St
Ninian's. Certainly there were times when he felt that
nothing was happening, nothing was working, and that he
was a failure and a useless servant. But this black mood
or depression did not normally extend beyond himself; no
one was caught up in his fog or gloom. He continued
praying, working and living hopefully. Others gained
confidence and trust from him, even though he might be
in the depth of depression.

Finally, Jock made the decision that he would seek a
release from his archbishop, so that he could give up the
leadership of the St Ninian's parish community. He wanted
to be free from the weight of administration. He knew he
had only so much energy to give, and he wanted the gift
to be of himself to God and of himself to leading people in
knowledge and love of God. The parting from St Ninian's
was not easy; for him it was a real bereavement. But he
felt he had helped to lead the community to a maturity
from which they could grow steadily. His decision was
founded very much on the attitude of St John the Baptist:
'He must grow greater and I must grow smaller' (John
3.30). He uprooted himself from the ten years of St
Ninian's. He took some of his possessions back to his family
home at Leuchie, the rest to his new appointment with

Father Charlie Barclay at Kirkcaldy. Only a few days before he made his final journey to America, he wrote to me of the emptiness of giving, the freedom of release and his profound gratitude which had given him the scope to live out the little way of spiritual childhood. For me it will always be a touch of Theresian closeness to the merciful love of God that Jock had his wish fulfilled of 'dying' on a golf course playing a round with a friend. I do not think I am being over sentimental or extravagant when I feel that, like St Theresa, he will spend his heaven doing good on earth. Indeed, I already have indications that this is so.

St Mary of the Angels   MICHAEL HOLLINGS
London W2

Part 1

Sharing in the Divinity
of Christ

1

Personal Holiness

Relationships

Martin Buber said, 'All real living is meeting'. Man is what his relationships are. They define him, make him the sort of person he is, are his life. Without any relationships we would not be human beings at all, but mere things. Imagine the difference between leaving three tables in a room for a week and leaving three human beings together for a week, and you will see the difference, and so understand what constitutes a man.

We have three basic relationships: to other men, to God, to self. Holiness consists in allowing these relationships to develop in the most human possible way and letting them be controlled according to the will of God. As a human being grows these relationships will develop anyway. Seeing that that growth is humanly healthy and in accordance with the Gospel is the business of sanctity.

With regard to our relationship with our neighbour the Gospel gives us the challenge of loving every other human being, friend and enemy alike. We have to remain open and with a 'heart of flesh' towards all, and avoid letting stony barriers be erected by our fears. There are all sorts of barriers which our fears erect between ourselves and other people. Laziness and self-centredness is one: we just cannot be bothered to be involved in other people. Envy or jealousy is another: a particularly ugly form of self-centredness. Anger is a third: both the quick spurt of hatred which alienates others from us, and the slow, smouldering sulks we all like to indulge in. The reader can think of other barriers. They are all obstacles to the flow of love between man and man. Another kind of obstacle is the external differences which exist between human beings and which present a challenge to love to overcome. They are the differences of age, temperament, class, race, colour, ideology. These barriers are not to be pulled down (thank God for our differences and the human variety they manifest), but they do make love more difficult.

A healthy human development means that as we grow closer in love to our fellow human beings we also grow in our love of God. We have a separate relationship with God, closely connected to our relationship with other men (the connection was made explicit by Jesus many times in the Gospel), but distinct. This relationship has to be itself developed. This is done chiefly by prayer: the one-to-one relationship, or encounter, with God. Here too there are obstacles of laziness, self-centredness and fear to be overcome. They are best overcome not by analysis but by simply entering into prayer. Face to face with God we grow in our openness to him. Prayer takes many forms. Usually we begin by asking God for things we want: petition. But the relationship goes deep when we pass from petition to thanks – saying sorry – loving – celebrating – adoring. Our 'rapport' with God is scarcely anything but superficial till we have developed a mutual relationship of love and spending time together.

Together with our relationships to God and neighbour, our relationship to self will grow. As we learn to know God and men, and to love them, we find ourselves going deeper in self-knowledge and confident self-affirmation.

Theology

To help us in the above growth, which is truly human, we have the teaching and example of Jesus Christ, that most human of men. The four gospels especially provide an inspiration for men and women to grow in their three basic relationships – to God, to other people, and to self. The teaching of the Sermon on the Mount and the life and death of Jesus are 'words' from God which express this sublimely.

Jesus did not leave only an ideal and an example to be followed. Being Son of God as well as man, he reunited the human race to God and remains present as Redeemer in this world, though invisible. Furthermore his followers have the privilege of being 'mysteriously' (i.e. sacramentally) united to him, like the branches of a bush to the parent stem. Initially in baptism, progressively in the Eucharist, Christians can grow closer to the person of Jesus Christ. This union with the person of Christ is mysterious and difficult to understand. But it is real. Another way of describing it is to say that Christians are given the gift of the Holy Spirit to energize their Christian development and lead them into all truth and closeness to God. The work of the Holy Spirit is precisely to promote and support the threefold development of human relations outlined above. We grow towards the Father in prayer, towards men in charity and ourselves in maturity by the power of the Holy Spirit. The visible reality seems purely human, but that is only the tip of the iceberg. The invisible presence of God's Holy Spirit is the major element, discernible to the eyes of faith only.

Growth

The Christian *mise en scène* is therefore the presence of the Holy Spirit in each baptized person enabling that person to grow in relationship to other people, to God, to self. The more the person grows in those three ways the closer he or she will be to sanctity. To facilitate this growth, Christians through the ages have developed a variety of practices, which can loosely be called religious practices. To help us to love our neighbour, ourselves and God, we practise daily prayer, examination of conscience, various 'devotions'; we may submit ourselves to a personal rule of life, make a habit of reading the Bible every day, say the rosary, go on pilgrimage, have a spiritual director, join a sodality. The Christian tradition has been fecund in producing a wide variety of these religious practices. Part of the growth towards sanctity is involving ourselves wholeheartedly in the practices we find most helpful. Another part, however, is the recognition of the need for detachment from those practices at the point when they begin no longer to help us towards God because they have become substitutes for God. Up to a point 'religion' helps the Christian to know and love God. After that point it becomes a 'golden calf', leading men into idolatry and away from God. That point is the moment for detachment even from religion in the interests of Faith. It is the moment when we have to be clear that religion is to be used 'adjectivally', not as a noun. Worship and adoration belong to God only, not to his creation, however religious. We must worship and cling unconditionally to God, not to our rule of life or to anything else. Otherwise we will be guilty of making the relative absolute, as the Scribes and Pharisees of Jesus' day did with the Law.

Mystery

The growth towards sanctity will, especially, involve a radical detachment from the words, concepts and theology surrounding our knowledge of God. Prayer leads us straight into the heart of mystery where we find that words fail, concepts no longer help, knowing gives way to unknowing. At this point man is no longer in control and is therefore insecure and 'lost'. If he does not turn back at this point in order to regain control, but perseveres into the cloud of unknowing, he will be rewarded with the peace that passes understanding and the experience of being grasped by God. Then all the three relationships he started out with remain, but coalesce in a marvellous way. He becomes one with himself, with God and with God's creation. That is what God intends to happen to us all. In the Christian vocabulary: 'This is God's will, your sanctification.'

2

Conversion

God as real

Christian conversion takes place when a man or woman
who has hitherto led a routine religious life suddenly
realizes that God is real. Conversion can take as many
forms as there are Christians, but common to them all is
this coming alive of the relationship between the person
and God. What up to then was an impersonal, slightly
routine, rather notional, not much regarded acceptance
that God exists and Jesus Christ his Son is our Lord,
suddenly becomes very real indeed and deeply personal:
Jesus Christ is seen as a Person in one's life, with whom a
living relationship is, 'incredible to relate', possible! That
being so, Jesus' relation to me and my relationship to
him immediately are seen as utterly the most important
relationship I have. Whether I am married or single, my
friendship and love for God becomes the most real of all
my relationships. He becomes the centre of my life and,
because he is other than me, outside of my personality, I
now have a new orientation away from myself. I begin to
live for God, not for self: away from myself and towards
the Master of my life, God. Everything else in my life, my
family, my work, my recreations, my interests now become

subordinated to this new, infinitely precious and important, relationship I have with God. Whether I give those secondary things up (and some do get given up under the impact of conversion), or whether I retain them, they are now seen in a new light, the light of my new link with God, and are judged and adjusted accordingly. It is not that they have become of no importance to me. On the contrary, in a certain way they have become more important. It is just that I now see and judge them completely in the light of the new meaning God has for me. He means everything to me now, from waking up in the morning to going to bed at night. In other words I have fallen in love with God.

A feature of those who have undergone the experience of being converted is that they look back to their life before it happened and wonder how they managed to call themselves Christians at all. They remember how they used to recite prayers like the 'Our Father' in a routine way with scarcely any meaning in them, and are filled with remorse for their former carelessness. Now prayer means so much. Before it meant so little. It is as if scales have fallen from their eyes, and they begin to see everything in a new light and with the warm glow of love: going to Mass and confession, helping neighbours, being self-disciplined, communing with God. Quite simply life has been transformed and, looking back, life before conversion seems to have been only half a life, a time of preparation for real living, not real life at all. A less happy feature of this transformation is that newly converted people, in the wonder of what has happened to them, can give the impression that they alone know what Christianity is about and can, usually unconsciously, seem to despise those who have not had the same experience as themselves. The zeal of the recently converted is not always tempered with sensitivity for others. If unchecked it can topple over the fine edge between enthusiasm and pride.

Conversion usually happens to people who have had close acquaintance with Christianity by being faithful members of the Church. When members of the Church undergo conversion their relationship to the Church is both the same and different from what it was before. They remain loyal members of their communion and usually become more committed to it as a result of their spiritual transformation, but there is a difference too – their focus of interest and love shifts away from the Church to the person of Jesus Christ. They realize, as if for the first time, that 'Christianity is not an it; it is a him'. What interests them, makes them tick as Christians, is not 'the Church' but Christ. Jesus is now the centre of their interest and love. The Church (e.g. the parish, school, convent, hospital) is no longer the chief thing they live for, devote their lives to. That position is occupied by Christ. They prefer now to describe themselves as disciples of a Master, not members of an institution. The difference may not show itself much on the surface, but it is very real in the psychological and spiritual sphere.

There are as many types of conversion as there are Christians. Although the common experience of all is this coming alive of the relationship to God, the way this is understood, or happens to the convert, is enormously varied. For some, what happens is a new realization of the fatherhood of God. This is how conversion worked in the life of St Thérèse of Lisieux. For her the fatherhood of God was the overwhelming truth of her life. Round that she constructed her Little Way of Spiritual Childhood. Someone coming in to her cell one day found her wreathed in smiles and ecstatic contentment. Thérèse explained that she was thinking how sweet it was to call God Father. For other converts Jesus Christ is the central figure. Clearly this is how St Margaret Mary Alacoque was set alight, with her vision of the Sacred Heart. Jesus Christ is also central in the experience of those Christians in Latin America who have been fired by the gospel imperative to liberate the oppressed. For them the promotion of the kingdom of God announced by Jesus Christ is what makes them tick. Jesus is for them the Way, *el Camino*, for them to follow, in numerous cases to modern-day martyrdom. Yet a third type of Christian is converted under the inspiration of the Holy Spirit and his gifts, and will describe the process as baptism in the Spirit. This is how it happens for those involved in the Charismatic Movement – sometimes so vividly that they think there is no other way to be converted and will expect baptism in the Spirit for all. Once again the zeal of the convert has produced tunnel vision which in time should give way to a broader, more understanding, view about how God acts in others whose experience has been different.

Spiritual experience

Conversion is practically always accompanied by a subjective experience of intense wonder and joy. Descriptions of this by those who have undergone it tend to give the impression that it is instantaneous and cataclysmic. In some cases it is, but in others the process takes place in slower motion and is prolonged over months, even years. The fact that joy does not last and is followed by the more humdrum experience of dryness and duty which acts as a test of its authenticity should not take away from the reality of the experience at the time of conversion. There is a considerable literature on the subject. William James's *Varieties of Religious Experience* (1901) is still the best survey;

the reader who wants to go further is recommended to read James's classic.

One aspect of the experience of conversion is the subjective feeling that everything in the person's life has 'come together'. Where before there was conflict in the self, between the demands of the lower and the higher appetites, between duties to self, family, friends, society, between this or that ambition, resulting in many false starts and contradictory emotions, after conversion unity reigns. The conflict between the higher and lower selves is resolved in favour of the higher self (St Paul's experience of this is described in Romans, chapters 7 and 8). The bewildering variety of choice with regard to duties somehow no longer seems bewildering but simple (though still demanding), because a way forward has been indicated and a goal set. The magnet of Christ has created a pattern in the confusion of iron filings which now easily fall into place round their magnetic centre. Or, to change the metaphor, the jam of logs in the river is broken and the current flows freely and fast in one direction towards the sea. The result is a welling up of joy and relief as the bits and pieces of one's life come together in harmony and peace. One experiences the rich harmonious fulfilment which the Hebrews called '*Shalom*'.

The overwhelming experience in conversion is that of joy. Pascal underwent a conversion to Christ at a precise time and place which he never forgot: he preserved his 'Memorial' of it written down and sewn into his clothing until he died. Perhaps the most moving line in it is the simple statement: 'Joy, joy, joy, tears of joy.' Statements like that could be multiplied from all the Christian saints. A welling-up from the inside in an ecstasy of joy is the common experience. 'All my feelings seemed to rise and flow out; and the utterance of my heart was "I want to pour my whole soul out to God". The rising of my soul was so great that I rushed into the back room of the front office, to pray,' – is a typical statement, which comes from the American Protestant revivalist C. G. Finney, describing his conversion. In St Luke's Gospel, chapter 1, there is an earlier statement of the same thing, which is familiar to all Christians: 'My soul magnifies the Lord, and my spirit rejoices in God my saviour.'

A third element in the conversion experience is the feeling of utter security in God. This is often a new experience for the recipient, since conversion usually follows a painful period of muddle and lack of purpose in life. The feeling of complete trust in God is a marvellous surprise, and remains a potent memory when times get hard again and anxieties and fears come flooding back. The fact that once I knew with certainty that God loves me and is infinitely trustworthy, sustains me through all subsequent trials and doubts. Another line in Pascal's 'Memorial' is: 'Certainty, certainty, heartfelt, joy, peace.' Sewn into his shirt, that stayed with him for life.

We respond to the gift of peaceful trust in God by surrendering ourselves wholeheartedly to him. Probably we will have been attempting to do this all our life. After all, to say the 'Our Father' is just that: 'Thy kingdom come, thy will be done'. At the time of conversion this surrender to God suddenly takes over. It becomes the blindingly obvious thing to do and beautifully simple, if not easy. Here again the saints have left many examples of this act of surrender composed into striking prayers. Charles de Foucauld's prayer of abandonment is one:

Father
I abandon myself into your hands;
do with me what you will.
Whatever you may do, I thank you.

I am ready for all; I accept all.
Let only your will be done in me,
and in all your creatures –
I wish no more than this, O Lord.

In Pascal's 'Memorial', the corresponding line is:

Sweet and total renunciation.
Total submission to Jesus Christ and my director.

Gift

'You have not chosen me – I have chosen you.' Jesus said
that to his disciples at the Last Supper. It can stand as his
message to all his followers down the ages, for we do not
choose the moment or the manner of our conversion. It is
not something we initiate, but something that we receive,
often unexpectedly and without warning. As I have
explained above, the overwhelming psychological
impression of converts is that they have been acted upon
from without, have had something *done to* them, quite
outside their control. Man's part in the conversion process
is initially to receive. This is not only the psychological
truth, but is theologically correct as well. The message of
the Bible, Old and New Testaments, is that of covenant:
God's unilateral decision to create in the first place, then
to redeem his followers in love. His followers have to accept
this grace lovingly and are always free to reject God's
advances, but there is no question of man ever choosing
God or choosing to be converted into a disciple of Jesus
Christ. The doctrine of grace preserves that truth, strengthened by the official teaching of the Church. Human beings
do not find it easy to believe that. We are incurably active
and too ready to believe that we must earn God's love.
From time to time Pelagianism, the doctrine that we can

earn salvation by our own efforts, becomes strong in the Church and there is needed a prophet of grace, like Augustine or Martin Luther, to remind us of the biblical truths. The point of the conversion process is that it is the event in which for once ordinary, non-theological Christians become aware of God's prior love of them and actually 'feel' that they have been chosen and acted upon and not that they have been making the initiative. Not the least of the wonders of being converted is that I am made to feel as well as think the truth about the gift of grace. My heart and my head coalesce in understanding God's gracious covenant of love. The doctrinal truth is an important guarantee of the genuineness of the spiritual experience.

Some readers may think that I have stressed so much the work of God in conversion that I have left no room for man to be anything but passive. But human beings have a very active part to play in the work of conversion. Their part is active before, during and after the time of conversion. Before conversion we prepare for it by the traditional religious acts of prayer, fasting, almsgiving, unselfish love of our neighbour and self-discipline. It is true that at the time of conversion we are completely transformed by a Power beyond ourselves, and that most conversions provide a radical discontinuity with what went before. Nevertheless, it is also true that we can and should prepare for God's action in our souls by resolute effort. This self-formation by man before conversion does not *cause conversion*, but it paves the way, as it were tilling the soil in preparation for the sowing of God's seed in the soul. It is in fact unlikely (though never impossible) that God will visit a soul which has made no preparation for his coming.

After conversion does man remain inactive, letting God do everything? Far from it. The moment of conversion is a moment of new beginning in partnership with God. From then on, under the almost irresistible force of God's grace, the Christian finds himself or herself unbelievably active in prayer, charity and self-discipline. So far from allowing the Christian to rest on his oars, 'saved', the impact of conversion drives him to a level of activity which he had not considered possible before, as he takes on more intense prayer, more works of love, more ascetical exercises in the cause of the Beloved. The amount of active work a converted Christian can perform exceeds all expectations and has to be experienced to be believed. All this activity, however, is not done to earn salvation, but simply to manifest God's love to the world. It is done from the love that has been discovered by grace, and is a joyous celebration in gratitude.

MAN'S PART

Repentance

A universal feature of conversion is intense sorrow for sins. Following on from meeting God there comes the realization that we have led sinful lives in the past, not only by what we have done (commission) but also by what we ought to have done but failed to do (omission). The very mediocrity of our unconverted lives shows up as sinful and displeasing to God. We are filled with remorse, as the new light of intimacy with God plays upon our lives and makes us ashamed. Sinful actions and omissions, which hitherto we were able to live with easily, now strike us appalling; we find it hard to accept our past record. We feel like Judas flinging back the thirty pieces of silver to the priests when he realized the horror of what he had done. There is a direct link between the closeness we now enjoy with God and our sorrow for sin. We have been drawn closer to the light of God by prayer, and in that light our sinfulness shows up strikingly. If we had not come so close to God we would not be experiencing our sinfulness so painfully. This explains why the saints have made such extravagant claims about their unworthiness and bemoaned their past sins. To us it seems a trifle exaggerated, to say the least, when saintly people like the Curé d'Ars repeat their professions of sinfulness. We wonder how genuine they are. The answer is that they are completely genuine, because they are seeing their lives under the light of the Truth who is God. The fact is that the saints have got the correct perspective on sin, and it is we, the half-converted, who are still in the dark or half-light about ourselves. The experience of conversion is the beginning of our journey into truth about ourselves and the world seen in the light of God's love.

Conversion does not only lead to remorse over sin; it also brings with it a huge confidence in God as our saviour from sin. Remorse for sin by itself is crippling and can lead to self-hate and despair. This is what happened to Judas who, when he saw what he had done, could not live with the fact and killed himself in self-hate. The gospel message is the opposite of despair. It is a call to hope. Just because we have sinned but now are sorry, we are the prime objects of God's love. Jesus came to save repentant sinners. He was especially close to them, delighted to be with them, held them as his special friends. He understood that there is no one more loyal than the person who has offended a friend, realised that it was wrong, said he was sorry and been readmitted to friendship in reconciliation. This is the theme of the story of the Prodigal Son. It is also the theme of Jesus' dealings with his friends. Peter being reinstated as head of the apostles after repentance for his three denials is the inspiring example of how Jesus acts with all his followers. For the Christian the sins of his past life need not be a reason for a cautious approach to the future. On the contrary they act as the reason for being more confident about God by coming closer to him than if we had never sinned. The measure of our sorrow for sin is the measure of our hope for the future. This explains why the saints, though weeping for their sins loudly, have no doubts that God loves them and that they can be close to him and do great things for him. This double conviction about past sin and future achievement is the foundation of Christian conversion. But note that to omit the conviction about past sins and go straight to Christian activity is to miss the point of the gospel. As St Augustine said, 'The beginning of good works is the confession of bad works.' There is no bypassing repentance for sins.

Prayer

To turn to prayer after conversion is the most natural thing to do, for after all conversion is itself an experience of prayer, the sudden warming of the relationship with God in direct communication. No one who experiences conversion needs to be told to pray more. More and intense prayerfulness is the first way in which we change our lives under the impact of being chosen by God. What needs to be stressed is the importance of perseverance in prayer after the superficial effects of conversion have worn off. At first 'the roll, the rise, the carol, the creation' of being loved so tangibly by God is uppermost in our lives, and praying is ridiculously easy and delightful to do. Sooner or later, however, the psychological effects wear off and prayer becomes dry and difficult, no longer the thing we looked forward most of all to doing each day. It now becomes a

dry struggle. This is the important time for our growth
after conversion, when we are asked to prove that our love
of God is deeper than delight in surface warmth, when we
have to prove that we are not just fair-weather friends of
God but all-weather friends. Most people who have been
really touched by grace do persevere at this point. The
reward of their perseverance is the discovery that God is
more truly to be found 'in the desert' than in the garden
of superficial delights. Once we have overcome the temptation to give up prayer because it is no longer particularly
enjoyable, our prayer deepens rapidly. Soon we have no
desire to live on a prayer diet of sensational experience and
prefer to plod on without much tangible reward, because
that way we learn to give more than to receive, and to
live in the good pleasure of God, rather than by our own
appetites. 'In his will is our peace,' said Dante. Persevering
prayer shows us that that peace surpasses human understanding, not least because it both exists and grows in
situations which are far from attractive on the surface.
Prayer is meeting God, communicating with him, letting
him communicate with us. Paradoxically that happens
more authentically when we are feeling dry and have to
make acts of faith in God and hope in goodness than when
we are experiencing good times in prayer. In the latter
instance there is the danger that we may be mistaking the
gifts of God for the reality of God. God shows us the
difference in the desert of dull prayer, patiently persevered
in.

Conversion of life to Gospel standards

For a Christian conversion is not a happening which leaves
us changed but unattached. Christian conversion is conversion *to* Jesus Christ. As we have seen, it is a deeply personal

commitment to God and to his Son, Jesus. Now, it is not possible to be committed to following Jesus Christ without the whole of one's life being changed. Jesus made radical demands on the way of life of his disciples when they gathered round him in Galilee, and he still does upon his present-day disciples. This is perhaps the aspect of following Christ which is most underplayed. We think that by being faithful to prayer, church-going and keeping the commandments we can be true followers of Christ without the rest of our lives being much altered. How wrong we are! To be converted to Christ means to be converted to his values, in the whole of our life, and that in turn means constant dissatisfaction with the accepted standards of civilized Western society – dissatisfaction because the values on which society is built are very much less than those of Christ and the gospel. Conversion, in fact, is the moment when we see that as Christians we cannot belong to two camps, deriving our religious values from Christianity and our social values from the society around us. Conversion places us firmly in one camp, that of Jesus Christ. From now on we have to view the accepted values of society as belonging to the other camp and, in the final analysis, opposed to Christianity. Conversion rules out for ever the sort of compromise which the Church too readily makes with the world's social and political values. Another way of putting this is to say that conversion to Christ means that we can no longer regard our religion as the controlling element of our private lives, while leaving our public lives to be controlled by secular ideas. Christianity is about the whole of life – public, political, social, as well as private. The gospel makes that clear, for after all it was for his public, political impact that Jesus was put to death, not for his teaching on prayer and love.

It is easy to see how in the past Christians went wrong

in this matter. It was wrong in the eighteenth century for those engaged in the slave trade to be 'devout Christians'. Their devotions should not have been nourishment for their private lives while leaving their economic lives unaffected. Their devotion to Christ should have made them refuse to countenance the slave trade, however economically profitable and socially 'allowed'. It was wrong in the nineteenth century that the Industrial Revolution which grew through gross exploitation of the poor in England's dark, satanic mills was led by Christians. However 'devoutly Christian' their private and family lives were (they frequently built churches and contributed to church funds out of the proceeds of their exploitation) their business lives, which followed the iron laws of trade regardless of human life and well-being, were spectacularly unchristian.

What about the twentieth century? We too have to see that conversion to Christ's gospel means a radical break with activities which are less than Christian in their working, though accepted by our contemporaries. We have to question the values of our contemporaries in matters of medical practice (e.g. abortion), easy divorce, legislation whereby the rich get richer and the poor get poorer, worldwide multinational commerce, because it exploits Third World countries and oppresses their populations in the interests of cheap food for the First World, not to mention good salaries, and even fortunes, for present-day merchant adventurers. To put it in a nutshell, conversion makes us see that we cannot simultaneously serve God and Mammon, and because we are now totally committed to God we have to break our ties with Mammon and so shock our contemporaries. In other words prayer has ceased to be a merely private affair between me and God. It has forced me to question the society I live in and to be prophetic about it in the name of Christ. True prayer is not a holy hobby, a drawing-room pursuit, for those who have leisure to read books and be interested in their souls. True prayer is a meeting with God, who invariably sends us from prayer to renew the face of the earth according to the values of his son, Jesus Christ. In nine cases out of ten this leads to conflict. Prayer is not, therefore, a cosy pursuit, anymore than the teaching of Christ was easy. As Leonardo Boff has said, there was an element of *intimidation* in the demands Jesus made upon those he had chosen. After meeting him and being chosen, their lives could no longer be comfortable or socially acceptable. Conversion to Christ means a break with the conventional past (*metanoia*) and a deep-down reorientation of our whole lives. It is therefore an event which involves a good deal more than the psychological excitement and comfort with which it normally begins. It affects our whole lives, and is awesomely real and uncompromising. It offers no peace outside the gospel of Jesus Christ.

Love and justice

From the preceding section it will be seen that the most important thing in Christian conversion is not the psychological experience of grace with which it is inaugurated. More important is what the Christian 'does with his conversion'. The gospel answer to what we should do with our conversion is to be found in Jesus' description of our judgment by God (Matt. 25:31–46). The test of conversion will not be found in how we have felt inside ourselves. It will be found in how we loved our neighbour. What authenticates a person's conversion is not his or her subjective feelings, which can be misleading, but whether it has led on to a life dominated by love of neighbour. As St John of the Cross said, 'In the evening of life you will be examined in love.'

The true follower of Christ ought to try to love not only the neighbour he sees and lives beside. He ought also to look for the forgotten, hidden neighbour, whom no one remembers to love. This has always been true, but in the present age it is especially a challenge, because the conditions of twentieth-century living make it possible for well-off, comfortable Christians never to meet or see their less well-off, marginalized brothers and sisters who are in special need of their love. It is possible to live all your life in a respectable part of a modern city and never have to meet or be faced with the thousands of your fellow citizens who live in appallingly blighted urban areas where unemployment is high, vandalism and violence are rife, and families are devastated by drink, drugs and other forms of social instability. It is not enough for a well-off follower of Christ to live in harmony and peace with his geographically close neighbours, those birds of the same feather with whom he flocks congenially. He must remember and look for those marginalized neighbours who are also members of God's family. It is particularly on his love for the unseen neighbour, impoverished by the conditions of industrial society, that the follower of Christ will be judged in the evening of life. Jesus made it plain that our attitude to the poor was the crucial test of love. If that is true of the situation within our country, it is even more true of the situation in the wide world. The really poor members of the human family are those who live in the Third World. Two-thirds of the human race live in that part of the global village where people have not enough to eat (many daily die of starvation), have no proper shelter to live in, have no health care, have no material security at all. They too are our neighbours. To do something about loving them calls for a variety of things to be done. It is a complex problem, which no single person can solve, but which resolute Christians can do something about when they band together to pray and act. No one can be converted seriously to Christ and not be involved in loving the poor of our global village.

Do our poor brothers and sisters in the Third World live in poverty and starvation because of a natural accident, or because of human oppression? Are their sufferings accidental or man-made? This is an important question, because if the former is true then the main thrust of our Christian love will take the form of emergency aid, succour for the victims, charitable action in imitation of the Good Samaritan. This happens, in fact, when a natural disaster strikes somewhere in the world, for instance an earthquake. But if the sufferings of our Third World brothers are man-made, if they are victims not of disaster but of *oppression*, then our reaction has to be quite different. Our love will now take the form of work for justice, work to see that the man-made unjust situation is re-made in justice. Our work in love will now be not so much with the victims of oppression but with those who cause the oppression and, in particular, with the whole economic and political *structure* of our global village which produces oppression by its built-in spirit of plunder (multinational trading, working in cheap, unprotected labour markets, on expropriated land, backed up by armed force and political dictatorship). Faced with the facts of our global village our Christian love is forced to 'go political', if only for the simple reason that to do nothing about the present arrangement of economy and politics in the world is already political, for it is not a neutral act but one which by doing nothing to change injustice actually works in support of the unjust state of affairs. Christian love, in other words, is forced to take

24

sides in the worldwide scene. This is the inescapable fruit of conversion to Christ and his gospel. Pedro Arrupe wrote, 'It has been said that interior conversion does not suffice, that we are told to perfect and progressively reconquer our entire being for God. Today we must be aware that what we must reconquer and reform is our entire world. In other words, personal conversion and structural reform cannot be separated.' Archbishop Oscar Romero, in a homily given on 10 February 1979, a year before he was killed in San Salvador, said, 'Nowadays an authentic Christian conversion must lead to an unmasking of the social mechanisms that turn the worker and the peasant into marginalized persons.'

Recognition of the political dimension of Christian love has come late to Christianity. But not too late for the work of the Holy Spirit to take it over and let it flourish. If the Church and world were to last for, say, another 50,000 years, then the imperfect start of the first 2,000 years would be seen as regrettable but not irrecoverable. This reflection will help us to see that after faith and love, hope is the virtue that is most manifest in Christian conversion. Conversion floods us with God's grace and, in the fine phrase of St Paul, gives us 'the mind of Christ'. Imbued with that mind we are able to share Jesus' wonderful love with all mankind, by inspiring them with faith and filling them with practical hope. No religious leader has given so much hope to the world as Jesus Christ with his gospel. Christians believe that he did this because he was the Son of God, sent by the Father. The phenomenon of conversion is simply the experienced conviction that I too, as a Christian, am sent by the Father in the same mission with Christ and that I too, therefore, can fill the world with his hope and turn it upside down with his love. That prospect fills me with 'Joy, joy, joy, tears of joy'.

3

Not Peace but the Sword

Disturbance and comfort

It is an undoubted fact that Christian spirituality has a certain chameleon-like quality. In the ages of Platonic philosophy its predominant message was flight from the world: monks and anchorites were the heroes of the Church. In the Middle Ages the predominant feudalism produced a spirituality of knighthood and fealty to Christ as sovereign lord. In the age of the European monarchies the Deity was absolute king: for St Teresa of Avila God was 'His Majesty'. Then came the Enlightenment, and Christian thinking was slowly transformed into a critical, liberal pursuit for the truth without myths. The Catholic Church made a belated accommodation to the spirit of the modern age at Vatican II after the backtracking of Pius X, and our spiritual approach is now nothing if not enlightened and liberal. It is all the more ironic that just when Catholics have become accommodated to the European liberal spirit, the predominant world philosophy is changing into something less liberal and more aggressive as the teaching of Marx permeates world thought. The new spirit of the 1980s is more dialectical, uncompromising and conflictive than we ever expected in the heady, liberal 1960s.

There is no need for Christians to be ashamed of the adaptability of the Christian message to each intellectual age. It is, surely, part and parcel of the Incarnation. The Word was made flesh at a moment in history. God's truth thus subjected itself to progressive human analysis and understanding. This means that God's truth subjected itself to being questioned by men, and what we may, slightly cynically, call the chameleon-like quality of Christians may also be seen as the proper unfolding of the Christian message as the ages succeed each other. In one sense the incarnation was God's last Word to mankind with no further revelation to be expected, but in another sense the very finality of that Word which came to us in the gospel, means that we will endlessly question and analyse it, and constantly be seeing it in a new light, from all the possible angles provided by developing human philosophy. Hence, progress in human secular knowledge will have its impact upon progress in understanding of the Christian message. New questions will give new insights into the gospel. The gospel, of course, remains the same: God's final revelation to us about himself and us. But our understanding grows enormously as we ask questions that previous generations did not ask. Pope John XXIII called this successive analysis of Christianity 'reading the signs of the times'. Gustavo Gutierrez says, 'Every great spirituality is connected with the great historical movement of the age in which it was formulated. This linkage is not to be understood in the sense of mechanical dependence, but the following of Jesus is something that penetrates deeply into the course of human history.*

This rather lengthy introduction is by way of explaining why it is that in recent times our understanding of Jesus and his gospel has moved from gentle Jesus meek and mild,

---

* Gustav Gutierrez, *We Drink from Our Own Wells* (SCM Press, 1984), p. 26.

the man of peace, to a considerably more conflictive model, the opponent of the Pharisees, the one who came to bring not peace but the sword, the espouser of the cause of the poor, the man of divisions. Is this simply because 'conflict' is now fashionable, or is it, as I believe, because our age is sensitive to the positive values of conflict and struggle and so is able to discern that element in Christ's life where former generations were blind to it because they did not look for it? It has been said that Christ came to comfort the disturbed and to disturb the comfortable. He can be seen to be doing both in the gospels. Hitherto we have concentrated in spirituality on the former type of activity: comfort for the disturbed. Charismatic spirituality is a notable example of that. 'Do not be afraid', 'You are precious in my eyes', 'I have loved you with an everlasting love' – these are the sentiments which predominate at meetings of charismatics. There is much oil poured to soothe and heal the wounds of broken humanity. What notably is absent in charismatic spirituality is vinegar to disturb, that element of jolt and challenge which Christ also put into his preaching. Without that element, in equal measure, the words of comfort run the risk of being superficial, mere oiling of the surface without regard to the immense need for change which both individuals and society have to undergo before they can be truly Christian. To shout, 'Peace, peace,' too soon is inimical to the gospel of Jesus Christ and is, in fact, a false path leading away from real peace. We would indeed be false prophets if we gave our contemporaries Jesus' comforting words of peace without his disturbing words about truth and justice. If in this article I concentrate upon the latter message of conflict, it is because I know that that is the only way for the true goal of peace to be achieved and for the words of peace to make sense.

Growth through struggle

Here below no growth takes place without struggle and death. The caterpillar has to struggle, be defeated, before it becomes a butterfly. The adolescent has to struggle out of his or her childhood, let the child die, before adulthood is born. In the same way, spiritually, virtue is not easily won by any person, but only comes as the fruits of victory over vice. Although theologically it is a gift from God, phenomenologically it is an achievement against odds. Chastity comes after, not without, the struggle against impurity. Fortitude is for the fearful person who overcomes fear, not for the (non-existent) 'fearless' person. In other words struggle is the law of the growth in human affairs. The Church has always understood that and been quick to eradicate the, sometimes seductive, appeal of quietism for religious-minded people. Quietism has been condemned not because surrender to God is wrong, but because surrender to God is not the same as surrender to passivity, or the line of least resistance when confronted with evil in this world. Faced with evil, Christians must not give in, as if that were abandonment to God's will. They must actively fight against evil, take up arms against it, in themselves, and in society. The surrender element comes not in putting up with evil but in putting up with the difficulties, unpopularities, slanders, pains, even deaths, which are incurred when we enter the struggle against evil. Our surrender to God's will makes us passive to his Spirit but fiercely active and combative in carrying out the promptings of that same Holy Spirit. As de Caussade said, 'When the Divine Order causes us to act, holiness is in activity.'*

Conflict with evil, then, is central to Christian spiritu-

* Jean-Pierre de Caussade, *Self-abandonment to Divine Providence* (Fontana, 1971), p. 20.

ality. Does this mean conflict with persons? Do we have to take up a hostile attitude to fellow human beings, fight against them, in following Christ? Are Christians sometimes commanded to be unpleasant to people, or should we maintain an attitude of sweetness and light at all times to all people? The short answer to this is to notice that Jesus was hostile and thoroughly unpleasant both to his friends at times ('Get behind me, Satan') and to his enemies, the Pharisees, a lot of the time. We should note, too, that he had enemies. In other words Jesus saw that being faithful to his Father's will to usher in the kingdom of God, a kingdom of love, justice and peace, meant a constant struggle not only against the 'forces of evil' abroad in the world, but also against the persons who, in his judgment, were fighting on the wrong side, for evil and against good. So he unashamedly and vigorously attacked people with his tongue, marshalled his followers against them and what they stood for, even used a whip to drive erring folk out of the Temple. He saw no contradiction in telling his followers to love their enemies but at the same time fight against them. In Jesus' teaching love was absolutely central, but love was not a business of surface smiles and patience, but rather of deep-down love which on the surface could take the form of impatient hostility. In this Christians have too often failed, and have reversed the order of priorities, being all smiles on the surface and all malice below it, thinking themselves truly Christian in doing so. I have encountered religious communities where the surface of the communal life was beautifully polite but deep down was seething with mutual enmity, and when I temerariously pointed this fact out I received the same treatment: surface politeness continued but the knives were out below it.

The answer to the conundrum of loving our enemies lies,

I suggest, in recognizing that the forces of evil are most of the time embedded in the structures of society, rather like woodworm in the furniture; and when we denounce evil in people we are not denouncing them as fellow human beings as such, but as victims of evil. We denounce them both to eradicate the evil which they are supporting, and to save them, our temporary enemies whom we love, from that evil. The only way we can get at the evil is often by denouncing the people who propagate it, but the real enemy is not the person who has embraced the evil, but the evil, unjust way in which human society is structured. The real enemy is structural evil, the 'sin of society' denounced by Pope John Paul II. That is how Jesus acted. He did not fight against the Pharisees and Scribes themselves so much as against the appallingly unjust and unspiritual way in which Jewish religion was officially interpreted, the godless paths into which it had run. In the same way when Christians in the world denounce Ronald Reagan for his murderous policies in Central America or Piet Botha for his oppression of South African blacks, we are not denouncing, still less hating, those two persons; what we are denouncing is the awful system of oppression which exists; for we know that should Reagan or Botha die tomorrow the oppression will go on with new 'presidents' in charge. Like Jesus, however, our denunciation has to be against identifiable leaders in order for it to be embodied and real. But like Jesus, too, it ought to be conducted from start to finish in love.

Conflict in the Church

There are at least four reasons why conflict in the Church is a good thing. Firstly because conflict is often the only way in which injustice can be tackled. People gently point out the existence of an unjust state of affairs, but it is usually only when they become hostile and actively campaign for justice that they are taken seriously. The advocates of women's rights in the Church understand this, as did the bishops at the Vatican Council on that second day when they revolted against the Curial 'arrangements' with which they were confronted. In other words, the gospel which we all try to serve is not about peace at any price but about peace as the fruit of justice and love, the Hebrew *shalom*.

Secondly, the gospel of Jesus Christ demands taking sides for truth and love, against evil. Diplomacy plays its part when the matter of conflict is neutral and mutual adjustment about morally indifferent claims is required. But there should be no diplomacy when one side is right and the other side is wrong. Does this ever happen? I think it does. Sadly there is an instinct in us all which tries to play the diplomat between sides which are not morally equal. Twenty years ago I was sometimes involved in the pastoral oversight of young priests just out of the seminary. The chief area of agony, and therefore of conflict, for those young men was that they had been taught the insights and ethos of Vatican II in the seminary and then found themselves with parish priests who had set their face against Vatican II and, incidentally, had usually not read a single thing about it. The bishop was brought in to mediate, which was his job. Too often the bishops would play the diplomat and urge accommodation on both sides. 'Learn to live together in love,' was the reiterated message, as if both sides of the conflict were equally weighted. But the conflict in question was not about a neutral matter, but about being for or against the Vatican Council, and the bishops' plain duty was to side with the young priests against the theologically illiterate older priests. A few did, but many did not. They voted in Rome for the Council measures but back in their dioceses baulked at the conflict involved in implementing those measures. They came from a generation which saw no good in conflict and in all sincerity sought to play it down. Their words were nearly always enthusiastically in favour of the Council measures but their deeds fell short because of fear of conflict. This disillusioned not a few young priests in their dioceses.

A third reason why conflict is good for the Church is because the Church has to be *semper reformanda* and, human nature being what it is, reform is seldom undertaken by those in power without first of all open discussion, and then some battling. It is seldom easy for those in authority to see reformers as loyal, but in fact they are nearly always deeply loyal people who care enough about the institution they belong to to want it to be better. In my days as a university chaplain I used to have to force myself to be warm to those reforming students who frequented the chaplaincy with radical plans to reform me, the chaplaincy and the Church. I had to stop myself classing them as disloyal. They were in fact very loyal and cared greatly about our Mother the Church. But sometimes I dreaded their appearance and found myself preferring their less loyal, more docile companions who did not care enough about the Church to want to reform it, and so did not upset me. A visiting prelate who had been given a rough ride by my flock commented, 'I wouldn't have your job for anything. I'd shoot the lot!'

A fourth reason for risking conflict in the Church rather than postponing confrontation is that a stitch in time saves nine. In the history of the Church how often disasters could have been avoided if the need for short-term conflict had been recognized and faced, so that reform could be implemented in time. The history of the sixteenth-century Reformation is largely a history of 'too little, too late', the besetting sin of traditional institutions. I believe that it is fear of conflict itself rather than fear of its outcome which makes us shy away from needed reform. Often we want the reform but cannot face the struggles involved in getting to it. An unworthy attitude for a disciple of Jesus Christ.

Conflict in society

If there is need for the recognition of healthy conflict in the Church in order to help it to be a fit instrument of God, there is even more need to recognize the need for conflict which we Christians may have to engage in as we do Christ's work in the world. Our task is not to be good Catholics in the Church but, following Cardinal Suenens' lead at Vatican II, to be good Christians in the world. In that work we have to accept that struggle with evil is paramount and completely unavoidable. In a short article like this it is not possible to delineate adequately the place that evil holds in our world and the inescapable element of clash with evil which discipleship of Christ brings with it. The Latin American theologians, from within the battlefield, have alerted us all to the centrality of this conflict. For them, and for us, the first step in *announcing* the Good News of the gospel is *denouncing* the evil that is in society. This makes enemies; and you are in conflict straightaway. The path to peace and justice is through unpopularity and persecution.

Not only do individual Christians have to embrace struggle with the powers of evil, but so does the Church as a whole. A notable development in the last twenty years in our country has been the way our Church leaders have passed from fighting for the rights of the Church in Britain (e.g. Catholic schools, exemption of clergy from military service) to fighting for human rights for all. Cardinal Hume lobbies the government over the arms trade and South African apartheid; Archbishop Worlock joins his Anglican colleague in a relentless fight with the government over unemployment on Merseyside. They see this sort of work as part of their task as bishops of the Church. A revolution is in fact quietly taking place in the Catholic mentality *vis à vis* the 'establishment'. As an immigrant Church we were distressingly anxious to get on well with the powers that be, were not above kow-towing at local and national level to the rich and influential, and showed disproportionate pleasure if Catholics were seen in high places. Now that we are more self-confident we can begin to rejoice that as a Church we are independent of the state and of the establishment ethos. This makes it more possible for us to follow Christ in the difficult task of the 'preferential option for the poor', which is clearly seen in the gospel, but which since Constantine has been obscured in the Church's mission.

An essential element in the struggle against evil is awareness. In our fragmented society, where modern transport enables the well-off to live in pleasant countryside while the poor and unemployed live in appalling housing estates rife with the drug trade and violent muggings and stealings, it is not easy for these different members of society to be aware of each other. Out of sight can mean out of mind. We do not see the people whom, by our very way of life, we are exploiting. In Jesus' parable of the rich man and Lazarus, at least the two protagonists met each other every day. That was the rich man's sin. He passed Lazarus every day but did nothing to help him. Modern society has altered the scenario. The rich man lives miles away from

Lazarus; they never meet. Does this make the former's sin greater or less? Perhaps the rich man's personal sin is less, because his day passes without a conscious decision to ignore the poverty of Lazarus. But the 'sin of society' is greater, precisely because it has insulated the rich from the poor, so that they need never meet nor think about each other. When you consider that this parable has a worldwide application, you can see even more the need for awareness. It is not just that business men who commute from Wiltshire to their London offices never meet the unemployed living in rotting housing estates in Teesside. It is that we in affluent western Europe never meet our starving fellow members of the human race in the Third World. But we depend on them. The brightly packaged cheap commodities, sugar, tea, coffee, chocolate, on the shelves of our supermarkets are one end of a chain which leads through multinational trading companies to the other end of the chain which is exploited, underfed, illiterate 'labour' in Third World countries miles away. We can, for instance, eat bananas galore for next to nothing in Europe because in places like Honduras the banana plantations are owned by a few North American companies who have taken the land and developed it for their own purposes, while Hondurans starve.

After awareness comes action, action to alter the structures of our world, because it is not individual sins which cause the glaring injustices of our world which cry out to heaven for vengeance. If it were it would be easy to tackle. What is needed is collective action on an international scale to combat the situation, alter the structures and make a better world. It is a hugely daunting task, so huge that many understandably draw back from it. Suffice to say here that, whether we draw back from the task or embrace it with prayer, the element of conflict will be centrally involved.*

Mystical union

The last point that needs to be made is to note that the call to combat and struggle by Christians in the world today is not a concession to imperfect people in an evil age, as if a more mature Christianity would feel no need for conflict. On the contrary, it is the very stuff of the gospel and the direct result of union with God by baptism. When we are baptized we are given the gift of the Spirit, united deeply with the risen Christ. Thereafter the spiritual life is an unfolding and a development of this deep union with God, and it is meant to result in mystical union. It is a great mistake to think that mystical union with God means being elevated above the human struggle into some sort of detached seventh heaven where we are no longer

* 'The Spirit of God enabled the prophets to feel with God. They were able to share God's attitudes, God's values, God's feelings, God's emotions. This enabled them to see the events of their time as God saw them and to feel the same way about these events as God felt. They shared God's anger, God's compassion, God's sorrow, God's disappointment, God's revulsion, God's sensitivity for people, God's seriousness. Nor did they share these things in the abstract, they shared God's feelings about the concrete events of their time. You could say that they had a kind of empathy with God which enabled them to see the world through God's eyes. The Bible does not separate emotions and thoughts. God's word expresses how he feels and thinks. The prophets thought God's thoughts because they shared God's feelings and values. This is what it meant to be filled with the Spirit of God and this is what enables one to read the signs of the times with honesty and truth. This too is what mystical union with God means.' Albert Nolan OP, *Biblical Spirituality* (Order of Preachers, Southern Africa, 1982), p. 23.

interested in this world. That may be the case in non-Christian mysticism, but Christian mysticism is union with the God of the Old and New Testaments, a God who is not aloof from this world but present in it and intensely interested in what goes on, committedly for good and against evil. Christian prayer unites us with that God, gives us, in St Paul's telling phrase, the 'mind of Christ'. This means that the Christian mystic will see the world as God sees it, nay, feel about the world as God feels about it. How does God feel about the World? Intensely compassionate and sad about those who are oppressed, intensely angry about the oppressors, intensely thirsty for sinners to repent, intensely in love with all his creatures and desirous of their turning away from sin and back to him in free love. Prayer gives us those same thoughts and feelings in our limited human way, and therefore impels us towards combat when we have to fight, and towards reconciliation when we have to be reconciled. Especially it gives us a maturity of judgement which will ensure that we do not fight simply for the sake of fighting, out of unregenerate aggressiveness, but will enter the conflict against evil with love in our hearts and always reluctantly.

4

Dying before Death

Passover pattern

In December 1982 I had a heart attack in the middle of
the night and was carried off to the coronary care unit of
the Western General Hospital. Three days later I had a
second, more severe, attack and became very weak. I lay
for a week in a state of suspended animation, not eating,
not wanting to read, or even think, with visitors limited to
five minutes at a time, 'living and partly living', thoroughly
ill. I learnt later that my family, who mysteriously
appeared at my bed from far away, were told I only had
a 25 per cent chance of living. For myself I thought I would
die, but curiously enough I did not dwell on this much,
firstly because I did not want to be a bore, over-dramatic,
with my family and, besides, could not find the right words
to speak about it. The main reason I kept quiet about
death, however, was because I had no 'imagination' to
think into the future. I was living entirely in the present,
concentrating on the struggle to live each moment against
a failing heart and, quite simply, had no energy to think
beyond each present moment. Consequently I was filled
with neither fear nor joy in thinking about my impending
death. About the future I found myself surprisingly numb.
All my thoughts were about *now*. Each moment, with
breathing proving difficult, took up all my attention. I can

remember, on the worst day, being submerged in waves of fear which were almost physical, and I can remember combatting these with the Jesus Prayer which I found helpful, not exactly comforting, but a sort of lifeline. I was certainly thinking about God, but entirely in the now, not at all in the future.

I have since had plenty of opportunity to think about that week in which I nearly died, because, thanks to the coronary care given me, I survived. I have had leisure to make some reflections and form some conclusions. My chief conclusion is that death is not important; what is important is dying. Furthermore, the important thing about dying is, actually, struggling against death, struggling to live. Living, not dying, is the focus of one's entire attention. So my reflections take the form of three convictions. Firstly that death is not important. It is not charged with meaning, but is merely the moment a person ceases to live, a very prosaic moment. My pastoral experience bears this out. I have been at many deathbeds. I have always found the moment when a person ceases to live extremely ordinary – the last breath, no more. Secondly, what we call dying is in fact living – living in a dying situation, diminishing visibly, but with a struggling reaction against the diminishment. Thirdly, this struggle as we die is charged with meaning, a great opportunity and challenge, worthy of all the attention paid to it by writers, poets and preachers. So I have reached the conclusion that when we talk about death and its meaning in the Christian understanding of things, what we really refer to is the struggle between life and death before death takes place, a struggle which is partly a surrender to dying and partly a fight against dying, a mysterious mixture of giving up and not giving up, of surrender and no surrender, in both aspects of which we encounter God.

One final thought, which is not a new one, but in fact a very traditional one: namely, we are dying all the time. As soon as we are born we begin to die. We live and grow, but all the time are marching inexorably to the end of life when we breathe our last. That being so, it is possible to interpret the whole of human life in terms of that mysterious mixture which makes up the experience of dying, the mixture half of which is a surrender to dying and half of which is a fight against dying. Our whole life consists in that series of experiences of death which are constantly being undergone and which lead to experiences of new life at a more mature level. This continuous series of dying leading to new life makes up the pattern of human existence, the passover pattern of growth into new life by way of diminishment and death. To put it another way, our life is made up of a succession of impoverishments which come as bad news each time, but when properly experienced lead to good news and enrichment. Between birth and death, then, our life seems to be made up of deaths and births! We undergo a continual procession of dyings which are followed by new births leading to new life.

I suppose it is true to say that this death–life process is a steady growth over all our lifetime, but it is also true that the steady growth is marked by special moments, definite jumps or jerks in the process, which stand out from the steady flow and which sometimes take on the aspect of crisis. If you examine your growth from childhood to adulthood you will understand what I mean. The transition from baby to child can be steady and almost imperceptible, but it also can be quite abrupt. This is even more true of the transition from childhood to adolescence which is almost invariably crisis-ridden. And so through life, as the teen-ager becomes an adult, the adult gets married (an abrupt change, however much foreseen and prepared for), the mother becomes a grandmother. All these changes are examples of the dying situations I have mentioned, which give way to a new birth, more or less gracefully, as the case may be.

The growing-up process provides many examples of how we have to die in order to reach the next stage of living. The child in us has to die before we become an independent teenager, and we do not become such until we have put away the cosy privileges and protectedness of the child. There is, incidentally, a parallel transition going on in the life of the parents who have to put away the protective attitudes appropriate to parents of a child and learn the new, more trusting activities appropriate to parents of adolescents. In few cases is this transition smooth and untroubled, so it is comforting to notice that Joseph and Mary also had a small crisis on their hands when Jesus began to show the independence of a teenager (Luke 2:41–51). But they got through it! For them as much as for us, it must have been a lesson in learning to die in order to be reborn, to be impoverished before being enriched. There is a charming poem by Cecil Day Lewis which well describes what I have been trying to say, pointing out how the crisis of growth is a lesson in love:

Walking away
FOR SEAN

It is eighteen years ago, almost to the day –
A sunny day with the leaves just turning,
The touch-lines new-ruled, – since I watched you play
Your first game of football, then, like a satellite
Wrenched from its orbit, go drifting away

Behind a scatter of boys. I can see

You walking away from me towards the school
With the pathos of a half-fledged thing set free
Into a wilderness, the gait of one
Who finds no path where the path should be.

That hesitant figure, eddying away
Like a winged seed loosened from its parent stem,
Has something I never quite grasp to convey
About nature's give-and-take – the small, the scorching
Ordeals which fire one's irresolute clay.

I have had worse partings, but none that so
Gnaws at my mind still. Perhaps it is roughly
Saying what God alone could perfectly show –
How selfhood begins with a walking away,
And love is proved in the letting go.

Another area of life where we successively die to be
reborn is that of parting. How poignant parting is; how
difficult it is! Personally I never get used to parting, either
from places or from people. Am I alone in having found
that it is just as sad to leave a place where I have been
unhappy as it is to leave a place where I have been happy?
In both cases, the places where I have lived and worked,
the house, the streets, the landscape twine themselves
round my heart like ivy round a tree-trunk. Every corner
has a memory which tugs at me to keep me from leaving.
'Partir c'est mourir un peu' (Parting is a small death). It really
is. Leaving people is, of course, even more difficult than
leaving places. I do not think John Henry Newman at
all overdid the poignancy in his sermon, 'The Parting of
Friends', at Littlemore in 1843. It is every bit as sad as he
said.

And, O my brethren, O kind and affectionate hearts, O
loving friends, should you know anyone whose lot it has

43

been, by writing or by word of mouth, in some degree
to help you thus to act; if he has ever told you what you
knew about yourselves, or what you did not know; has
read to you your wants and feelings, and comforted you
by the very reading; has made you feel that there was a
higher life than this daily one, and a brighter world than
that you see; or encouraged you, or sobered you, or
opened a way to the inquiring, or soothed the perplexed;
if what he has said or done has ever made you take
interest in him, and feel well inclined towards him;
remember such a one . . .

And yet we know that unless we part from one place and
stage in life we cannot begin in another. Our affection for
the first has to be released and purified before we can treat
the new place with seriousness and respect. So also with
colleagues and friends. However heart-rending the break
up of a partnership, it often has to happen, happen quite
brutally, in order that we can grow and work seriously
with new partners. To refuse to accept the death of a past
partnership can hamper for ever the making of new ones.
Here is certainly a case where growth 'begins with a
walking away, and love is proved in the letting go'.

The most difficult of all partings are those which are
not of our choosing, which happen to us involuntarily. A
voluntary parting is bad enough, when you have to move
on in the interests of work or development, leaving friends
behind. Involuntary parting is much more painful, when
you make no decision to leave, but find that others have
made it, and are leaving you. It is hard in these cases not
to feel a sense of rejection. Very often you have in fact been
rejected. The pain is sharp, even in humdrum cases like
having an offer of help brushed aside by a friend, or going
for an interview and not getting the job. Worse still, of

course, is the case of being rejected in love, having to accept that someone you love does not want you, having to stand by and watch while another is preferred. For young people this death is often the first experience of adult life for them; it comes as a heavy blow and they wonder if they will ever live through it, or be happy again. Older people also have their own experiences of being rejected when someone they love, a friend, a partner in marriage, dies. Bereavement to the elderly is often as much of a shock as being jilted is to a young person. It leaves us equally lost and empty of future hopes. It is a real impoverishment and has been described as like losing a limb. One is left facing the remainder of one's life without someone who has been as much part of that life as a leg or an arm. It is a death of part of oneself; but, once again, if properly accepted, it can lead to a spiritual enrichment unforeseen in happier times. I have known widows and widowers who have achieved new depths of Christian understanding and strength through this harrowing experience of bereavement. Out of their dying has come a resurrection.

The Christian mystery

For Christians this perpetual pattern of death–resurrection in their lives is given meaning by the life, death and resurrection of Jesus Christ. The passover of Jesus, the central story of Christianity, is a powerful myth which enables us to make sense of our lives. We tell and retell the story, dwelling on the dereliction of Gethsemane and Calvary, when all that humanly mattered for Jesus, his friends, disciples, his cause, his preaching, simply collapsed, died. The death on the cross was the death of everything for Jesus: he was truly 'forsaken'. Then we tell and retell the story of the resurrection, ascension and the descent of the

45

Holy Spirit at Pentecost and thrill to the news that, for Jesus' friends and disciples, cause and preaching all came back, risen and bursting with new life. This archetypal story of dying and rising again helps the followers of Christ to make sense of their lives. The Church knows this and in the liturgy tells and retells the story, for the first function of liturgy is to narrate to the people of God their foundation story, and to keep it alive in their collective memory. They meet liturgically to *commemorate* Jesus. In what happened to him we see hope and meaning for ourselves in the deaths and resurrections of our lives.

Liturgy, however, is more than just commemoration. Its impact is more than psychological. Because of the presence of the Holy Spirit in the Church and her sacraments, our link with Jesus is real. We are linked not only by the communal remembering of the passover of Christ, but also by the real presence of the risen Jesus in the Church and in her members. So, in some mysterious but completely real way, our little deaths and resurrections are joined across history to Christ's death and resurrection and his historical passover is in turn re-enacted in those little passovers of our lives. Christ's passion is not just a psychological thing, needing to be remembered. It is real, a strengthening grace needing to be received. This real presence of Jesus in the celebration (both of word and sacrament) is the heart of Christian liturgy. Romans 6 makes this plain. In liturgy Christ's passover is a real event in the present, as well as a narrative of the past.

Do you not know that all of us who have been baptized into Christ Jesus were baptized into his death? We were buried therefore with him by baptism into death, so that as Christ was raised from the dead by the glory of the Father, we too might walk in newness of life. For if we have been united with him in a death like his, we shall certainly be united with him in a resurrection like his. We know that our old self was crucified with him so that the sinful body might be destroyed, and we might no longer be enslaved to sin. For he who has died is freed from sin. But if we have died with Christ, we believe that we shall also live with him. (Rom. 6:3–8.)

Liturgy, however, is not the whole story. What goes on in my life outside liturgy is crucial. In liturgy I celebrate with the Church the victory of Christ over sin and death, once for all on Calvary and therefore in my life too (if only I allow grace to take me over). When liturgy is finished, however, I must go out into life and make real in the ordinary routine of my days what I have so solemnly celebrated in Church. The passover of Christ has only entered my life if all those daily passovers of mine are joined to it, strengthened by it. Liturgy without the life that precedes and follows it is an empty shell. This may seem an obvious truth, but it seems to me worth saying because, especially in my Church, you could be fooled by much of what is said into believing that our apostolate is primarily to create 'good liturgy' in our parishes, to have worthy sacramental celebration, meaningful liturgies of the Word. But Jesus himself followed the tradition of the Old Testament prophets in distancing himself somewhat from liturgical celebration, and making daily life lived generously the heart of discipleship. The beatitudes are prescriptions for everyday life, not rubrics for worship. Liturgy comes into its own as the celebration of the Christian passovers of our daily life. It does not stand by itself. We are saved by Christian living, not by Christian liturgy.

Paschal spirituality

How *do* we live the Christian passover? What is the best way to die in order that we may live? How should we handle the impoverishments of our lives in order that we may receive the enrichments? I suggested earlier that our reaction to these diminishments should be a mixture of surrender and no surrender. Getting the mixture right is always a problem and there is no 'correct' answer, but I suggested our reaction in these situations should be in two stages. The first stage is to fight against what is happening, to resist sturdily and refuse to accept. At the onset of illness we have to resist what is happening and want to be cured. If rejected by one we love, we must not give in, but fight against the rejection with all our strength. The proverb reminds us that faint heart never won fair lady! We must never have faint hearts. We have to fight for our friendships and partnerships. This initial reaction of non-acceptance has sometimes been understressed by Christian thinkers, but it is in fact the crucial difference between true Christianity and fatalism, between true mysticism and false quietism. It is, for some, seductive to give in to the onslaughts of opposition from events and people, but it is not Christian and does not lead to growth and maturity. It is, under analysis, the line of least resistance to accept a setback or an evil too quickly. It is not 'the cross'. The cross is what we suffer in the fight for good, not simply the acceptance of evil.

A second stage comes (don't ask me when!) when we find that we are not going to win our fight: the illness is incurable, our friend *has* rejected us. Then is the moment for surrender, for now we know that the will of God for us is to accept defeat, just as earlier on it was to fight against defeat. This second stage is, for some, more difficult than the first. It requires us to give in to God, not fatalistically with a shrug of the shoulders leading to bitterness and resentment, but sweetly and lovingly, embracing the humiliation involved. The cross now really is to accept setback and defeat and to do so humbly – just as to go on resisting God at this point is paradoxically the line of least resistance. New life now lies the other side of the death involved in accepting what God is allowing to happen to our life.

This very human, rather messy, mixture between fighting and surrendering is not easy to tabulate with clarity, but I am certain that both elements have to be present in Christian living if we are to live out the Christian mystery faithfully. In my analysis I have been greatly helped by Teilhard de Chardin's *Le Milieu Divin*. Here is an extended quotation:

> If he is to practise to the full the perfection of his Christianity, the Christian must not falter in his duty to resist evil. On the contrary, during the first phase, . . . he must fight sincerely and with all his strength, in union with the creative force of the world, to drive back evil – so that nothing in him or around him may be diminished. . . . Should he meet with defeat . . . he will, like the conquered pagan hero, still inwardly resist. Though he is stifled and constrained, his efforts will still be sustained. . . . But in the realm of the supernatural, as it is called, *there is a further dimension* which allows God to achieve, *insensibly*, a mysterious reversal of evil into good. Leaving the zone of human successes and failures behind him, the Christian accedes by an effort of trust in the greater than himself to the region of supra-sensible transformations and growth. . . . We must understand this well and cause it to be

understood: to find and to do the will of God (even as we diminish and as we die) does not imply either a direct encounter or a passive attitude ... I can only unite myself to the will of God (as endured passively) *when all my strength is spent*, at the point where my activity, fully extended and straining towards betterment, finds itself continually counter-weighted by forces tending to halt me or overwhelm me. Unless I do everything I can to advance or resist, I shall not find myself at the *required point* – I shall not submit to God, as much as I might have done or as much as he wishes. If, on the contrary, I persevere courageously, I shall rejoin God across evil, deeper down than evil; I shall draw close to him; and at that moment the optimum of my 'communion in resignation' necessarily coincides with the maximum of fidelity to the human task.*

So much for Teilhard de Chardin. The whole thing has, perhaps, been more easily put in the Book of Genesis in the story of Jacob wrestling with the angel (32:24–32). It is a story I find very moving. Jacob did not give in straight away to the man who opposed him. He fought *all night*. Only after that night of struggle did he give in, knowing now that it was God he was fighting against. Then he surrendered. He accepted defeat and asked for and received a blessing. The blessing is resurrection and new life after we have died. We have no right to think that this blessed new life ever comes to us cheaply without a fight.

The last stages

All the deaths and resurrections in Christ which we undergo prepare us for the last years of our life when the

---

* Pierre Teilhard de Chardin, *Le Milieu Divin* (Fontana, 1964), pp. 91–3.

focus of living is beginning to be more obviously preparation for dying. I have said that in one sense we are dying from the moment we are born. In the early parts of one's life this is little more than a piece of rhetoric. At some time after the age of fifty I think it begins to be more real. So in this last section I would like to look at the last years of life in the light of what I have already said about the paschal mystery. Growing old has many aspects. I would like to dwell on some of them and see how to make sense of them in terms of that surrender and no surrender mixture which is for us the living out of the mystery of Christ in everyday life.

As we grow old the body begins to fail. We are no longer able to do what we used to do. Physically we need more rest, more help from others. Occasionally we have dramatic illnesses which land us in hospital. More irritating are the daily little physical infirmities which never were before, but now are, part of our lives. How do we deal with these? At one level by fighting against them, not giving in too soon, determining not to become an invalid; but at another level by accepting the inevitable, lovingly as from the hand of God, and adjusting our lives accordingly with the minimum of fuss, humbly recognizing what is happening as an opportunity to grow closer to God. In this minor passover experience the Lord is offering us a lesson which we have to be humble to learn: Christian discipleship is not measured by external achievement but by the strength of love in the heart. Growing old teaches us that lesson, provided we allow ourselves to listen to it.

Our attractiveness for other people lessens. Younger people appeal to our contemporaries more. Our sexuality lessens, and with it a certain glow in our lives. The lesson to be learnt here is once again a middle path between giving up in despair and not caring at all for one's appearance or impact on people, and the equally ridiculous refusal to accept one's age by going on trying to be young. We have to accept that our youth has died for ever and will not be resuscitated; but once we have accepted that truth, the way is open for a mature old age which recognizes that we can help those around us precisely by diminishing and allowing others to shine. This new life, however, lies on the other side of a humble acceptance of diminishment.

All possible futures die. We wake up to the realization that we have only the life we have! The fanciful dreams of things we might do, places we might go to, fade away. This I have found to be a considerable death. I have always liked to think of alternative lives I could be living and alternative places I might go to! But it does not take much reflection to see that this fading of the dreams and fantasies of youth is an enormous gain in reality. This growth into reality is, of course, a growth into God, a real resurrection from the death of being young and unreal into true Christian vision. Paradoxically, old men who have experienced the destruction of the immature dreams of their youth are sometimes then able to dream real dreams of enormous power and truth. I think, for instance, of Pope John XXIII whose rigorous spiritual life prepared him for the impossible dream of the Vatican Council at the age of seventy-seven. What a resurrection that was after the death of middle-age caution.

Responsibilities tend to lessen as we get older. Grandmothers have less responsibility than mothers, retired people less than working people. When we are still working, we deceive ourselves into looking forward to retirement and the shedding of responsibilities, but if we have self-knowledge we know that it will not be easy to retire. We will miss being in the centre of things, of having our advice sought, of initiating policy and being creative. We will

soon find retired life dull after the anxieties and thrills of
leadership. Job experienced this and put it into beautiful
words with which many of us can, I am sure, identify:

> Oh, that I were as in the months of old,
>   as in the days when God watched over me; . . .
> When I went out to the gate of the city,
>   when I prepared my seat in the square,
> the young men saw me and withdrew,
>   and the aged rose and stood;
> the princes refrained from talking,
>   and laid their hand on their mouth;
> the voice of the nobles was hushed,
>   and their tongue cleaved to the roof of their mouth.
> When the ear heard, it called me blessed,
>   and when the eye saw, it approved;
> because I delivered the poor who cried,
>   and the fatherless who had none to help him. . . .
> I was eyes to the blind,
>   and feet to the lame.
> I was a father to the poor,
>   and I searched out the cause of him whom I did not
>   know. . . .
>
> Men listened to me, and waited,
>   and kept silence for my counsel.
> After I spoke they did not speak again,
>   and my word dropped upon them. . . .
> I smiled on them when they had no confidence; . . .
> I chose their way, and sat as chief,
>   and I dwelt like a king among his troops,
>   like one who comforts mourners.
>
> But now they make sport of me,
>   men who are younger than I,

whose fathers I would have disdained
to set with the dogs of my flock. . . .

And now I have become their song,
I am a byword to them.
They abhor me, they keep aloof from me;
they do not hesitate to spit at the sight of me.
Because God has loosed my cord and humbled me,
they have cast off restraint in my presence.

(Job 29—30)

Poor Job! He was suffering badly the pangs of retirement, the death of responsibilities. The Book of Job is, in fact, an eloquent lesson in that mixture of no surrender and surrender which is Christian discipleship. Job refused to accept that his losses were his own fault. He fought strongly against any suggestion that he should surrender to God out of guilt. But Job did surrender to God in accepting that what had happened to him was God's work, even though he was never told why. He did surrender from the first to the will of God. In the Old Testament he stands out as being close to the Christian understanding of suffering and setback, a kind of pre-Christian prophet of the paschal mystery.

There are, of course, other aspects of growing old which could be mentioned, not least the worst dying of all, when all our root certainties about religion, church, faith and God simply evaporate, and leave us unbelieving and empty. But that is for another occasion. I hope that by talking about life before death I have been able to speak profitably about life after death. We have no experience of that. In our hearts we do not know what lies beyond death apart from what the promises of Revelation say. But we do have experience that God keeps his promises about this life. Those kept promises help us to be assured that there is a continuity in God's dealings with mankind. All the little impoverishments and deaths of our life prove capable of leading to enrichment and new life. In dying to childhood, or good health, or human importance, throughout our lifetime, we find that under God we can be creative of new life, new depth, new enrichment even in this life. The promise is that when we come to die finally, if we accept our death faithfully, a new life, new depth, new enrichment of utterly inconceivable glory will be given to use beyond the grave. We pin our hope on that promise which is in line with all God's dealings with us so far. I do not think we will be disappointed.

5

Suffering in a Christian Perspective

There is nothing particularly Christian about suffering and sickness. They are the lot of all mankind. No human being escapes them, though some receive far more than their fair share during the course of one life. One thinks especially of the millions in the world (not just thousands) who go to bed hungry every night and whose children have no schooling, no health care, no future to look forward to. They, the majority of mankind, will never read a book like this, but we should not forget them even though I am here chiefly addressing myself to the suffering and sickness which we in western Europe and the USA have to undergo from time to time.

The Christian element in suffering comes not in the suffering itself (which men and women of all beliefs or none experience) but in the way in which suffering is received and handled. Followers of Jesus Christ believe that there is a specifically Christian way of tackling suffering when it comes into our lives. Although we do not always, or even ever, succeed in being fully Christian about pain and hard-ship, nevertheless we have an ideal to follow. The ideal is exemplified in the life of Jesus Christ and in the saints who have imitated him in their lives.

A common misunderstanding about the Christian atti-tude to suffering is to say that we should simply accept it uncomplainingly. The figure of Jesus on the cross is invoked as the supreme example of this attitude. 'He went to the cross without complaint, accepting his passion as the will of the Father for him. He offered it up for us.' Although much of this statement is true, there is a dangerous short cut in the argument. It would be more true to say that Jesus was killed on the cross because he fought against suffering and sickness, not because he accepted it. In fact he was persecuted and put to death because of his non-acceptance of suffering and sickness. In Galilee and Judea he was surrounded by people oppressed by suffering, some of it at the hands of men (like the priests and scribes who laid impossible burdens on the shoulders of the poor, cf. Matthew 23:1–39), some of it by natural causes, disease and mental anguish. All of it in Jesus' eyes was unnecessary. He fought against it. Confronted with disease and desperation, he healed people, affirmed them, taught them to have faith that their disabilities were not the Father's will and could be overcome. In like manner, when he came across the sufferings imposed on the poor by their religious leaders he took up arms against those leaders and fiercely castigated them for causing such suffering in the name of religion. Jesus in no way accepted that life for his contemporaries had to be full of suffering. He did his best to do away with it when he met it. This made him unpopular. He became a threat to the religious authorities, so they planned to kill him. It is here that we come to suffering in Jesus' own life. He knew that the course he was pursuing would lead him into trouble, and apparently foresaw the physical tortures he would be subjected to: scourging, crucifixion. Even here it is not true to say that he simply accepted them, because on many occasions he avoided confrontation with his enemies, taking refuge in neutral territory. It was only when he could no longer avoid confrontation without compromising his

principles that he saw that his death was the Father's will.
Then he accepted it, embraced it, offered it up for the
redemption of mankind. Accepting the cross was the last
move on Jesus' part in a campaign where all the previous
moves had been to do away with suffering and sickness.

To follow Christ in suffering means, then, to do two
things: to fight against it with all our strength and to accept
it with all our strength. There is clearly a paradox here, but
unless we stress both the fight against and the acceptance of
pain, we do not understand the full meaning of suffering
as Christ suffered. Both elements belong to the Christian
tradition, and both have to be stressed. The fight against
suffering takes the form of healing. Faced with the some-
thing-gone-wrong which we call sickness, whether it is
physical, psychological or social, the Christian action must
be to heal it. This means rejecting it, not accepting it,
striving to do away with it. This is what Jesus did. What
a travesty it would be to draw a picture of him going round
telling people just to accept their illness as from God and
do nothing about it! No, Jesus healed lepers, drove out
unclean spirits, reconciled the sinners of his society. In this
way Jesus inaugurated the noble Christian tradition of
caring for and healing the sick, setting in motion that
marvellous history of Christian hospitals and care for the
sick which have existed from his day to ours.

However, the Christian struggle against disease is not
the whole story. There is also the element of acceptance.
The true disciple of Jesus Christ does not rail against pain
and suffering. He or she recognizes it as a trial permitted
by God for his own mysterious purposes, and, even as he
or she sets out to be healed, accepts it full-heartedly. This
acceptance is not just a surface thing, but goes deep down,
and foresees and embraces the possibility of there being no
recovery, that death may be the outcome. This acceptance

calls for as much vigour of soul as the previous determination to fight the cause of pain. In both cases the enemy to Christianity is an easy acceptance of the line of least resistance. To give in to disease without any fight is the line of least resistance, but failing to accept pain is also the line of least resistance, because it is so easy to try to turn away.

You may perhaps wonder how to make sense of this contradictory advice both to fight against and to accept suffering. The truth is that we are in the presence of mystery when we encounter pain, so there is no facile solution to the problem of how to handle it. Perhaps a useful rule of thumb is to say that we should always begin by total resistance to suffering and always end by total acceptance of it. If we do not initially oppose it with all our strength we cannot hope to conquer it, that is, heal the disease, reconcile the quarrel, eradicate the evil. But at some point we must seek to recognize the element of God-givenness in the situation, and to that element we must give unqualified surrender. My experience of two heart attacks and my own reaction to illness has taught me something about Christian suffering, and at the time my reaction was largely instinctive, but I believe it was Christian instincts which I followed and which led to my recovery. On the one hand I resisted the happening, and struggled with all my (weakened) heart not to die. This, I am sure, helped the doctors and nurses in their task of restoring me to health. A patient who 'gives in' very often dies through lack of will to live. On the other hand I recognized from the start God's permissive hand in what had happened to me, and I think that this acceptance and my basic willingness to go to death if God wanted me, also helped the doctors. The patient did not despair or panic, but remained trusting the Lord throughout. Somehow I was led to the right sort of balance between submitting and refusing to submit to the illness which had come upon me.

So far I have stressed the need to follow the example of Jesus Christ in our attitude to suffering. Christians, however, have an even more wonderful truth to embrace than the example of Christ, and that is our living relationship with him by reason of the union between him and ourselves given by baptism. Jesus is not only a figure in the past whom we can imitate. He is, more especially, the risen Christ present here and now, into whom we are incorporated as members. In other words we not only suffer in imitation of Christ on the cross two thousand years ago; we are privileged to suffer now in union with him in all our day-to-day crosses. Our crosses somehow become his; his cross becomes our cross (cf. Rom. 6:3–4). This mystical truth has given strength to countless Christians in their suffering and illnesses and helped to make sense of the bafflement of pain. This pain cripples me in body and mind, but I am given strength in my bewilderment by feeling that Christ is with me in it. Like St Paul the suffering Christian can say: 'We are afflicted in every way, but not crushed; perplexed, but not driven to despair; persecuted, but not forsaken; struck down, but not destroyed; always carrying in the body the death of Jesus, so that the life of Jesus may also be manifested in our bodies' (2 Cor. 4:9–10).

As Christians the sufferings that we undergo help us to succour all others who suffer. Our attempts to bear sufferings in union with Christ and in imitation of him in his life and passion should give us the right approach towards our neighbours who are ill. It is not just a question of the attitude beneath the words we use, an attitude which on many occasions may prompt us to be silent rather than speak. In fact, silent empathy is, more often than speech, the best course for us to adopt in the sickroom. People who are ill do not need or want chatter round their bed, however well meant it may be. When you are in pain, with the mental muddle that pain so often brings, you do not feel up to listening to someone addressing you. On the whole, you want silence. On the other hand you very much want company and are afraid when left alone. So the best course for those who visit the sick is first to be present with the sick person. One's sympathetic presence may, of course, prompt one to perform actions of assistance and even to engage in conversation if the patient desires that. But the vital thing is just to be present and in sympathy. For many people, perhaps for most, this is a difficult thing to do. Our education has taught us to be busy and doing things, and we are often quite lost if we are asked just to sit and neither say nor do anything. It makes us feel 'useless', thoroughly uncomfortable, longing to be up and doing things to help. The rare person who can sit and be silent for hours at a sick bed is the one who helps most. Such a person is usually a man or woman of prayer.

Many have found that a most effective way of keeping present to a suffering person without saying anything is by touch. If you can hold the hand of the sufferer, or just lay your hands upon his arm, you can offer reassurance twice as effective as speech. More often than not the sufferer responds in the same medium by a pressure of the hand which is less tiring than having to speak. At the deathbed of a Presbyterian businessman, who was a master at presenting accounts at board meetings but who was almost inarticulate when it came to matters of the spirit, I was moved beyond words when he took my hand and stroked it just like a child looking for reassurance from its mother. From then on the communication between us was through

our hands, which said all that was necessary. Fear is the
enemy, the Devil's chief weapon, when people are in pain.
We can be of enormous use if we can help people to overcome their fears, or, at least, if we can accompany them
through their fears. The sense of touch is the most
reassuring of all the senses in the face of fear. Holding on
to our friends is the way we face and overcome fear.

It is in the context of all that I have said above that I
see the effectiveness of the Church's sacrament of the sick.
It is a beautiful service. It can be accompanied by meaningful passages from Scripture designed to help those in
pain. But it has to be administered with sensitivity – otherwise it will be just a rubrical observance of the correct
rites, no more. We therefore bring Christ into the sickroom
most effectively when we recognize the primacy of silent
empathy over words, even consecrated words, and when
we recognize that the touch of a pastor, who is also a
sympathetic friend, is needed to transform the words of the
ritual into the presence of Christ to the sick person. Study
the words of the ritual and use all its rich possibilities to
the full, but study first the mentality of a suffering person.
That sort of study is done by prayer and in the heart, not
in the head or in lecture rooms.

Part 2

Sharing in the Redemptive
Work of Christ

6

Liturgical and Private Prayer

Before attempting to discuss the relationship between liturgical and private prayer I should like to spend some time on the subject of prayer itself, because today there is doubt in many men's minds as to whether prayer as a distinct operation is a valid Christian act at all. I myself believe that it is and I hope to show this. The problem of prayer can best be approached through the problems of life rather than vice versa. Clearly 'prayer' and 'life' are intimately connected. The traditional way to see the connection between the two has been to talk first about prayer and then show how it overflows into the whole of life. It is, however, just this way of beginning with prayer which fails to satisfy people today, so that a better way to proceed is to talk about life and then try to show that what we call 'prayer' springs from the centre of Christian living and is part of it. The huge success with a widely diverse public of the books of Michel Quoist is proof of the value of this way of approach, becaus this is how Quoist approaches prayer: he starts with the ordinary things of life, blackboards, five pound notes, being jilted in love and goes from them to prayer. I am not saying that one cannot talk about prayer without first talking about life, but only that I do not consider it a very convincing way today.

The Christian life

Christian living may be summed up by saying that it is a threefold commitment, at each stage of which we are summoned by Christ to respond affirmatively, to say yes. It is a commitment to life, to people, and to society. First we are asked to say yes to life. I know this is a rather vague phrase, culled from the existentialists, but I think there is no doubt what it means. It means reacting to the successive challenges of life creatively, in a co-operative outgoing manner. Our instinct is often to withdraw into ourselves and refuse the challenge that a situation brings – this is to say no to life, and it is the opposite of the Christian attitude which is creative and co-operative. This saying of yes or no to life occurs in every situation from the ordinary ones like getting out of bed in the morning or opening unpleasant looking letters to the big decisive moments like applying for a job or solving a family crisis. In all these situations we can either respond affirmatively by facing the challenge, or negatively by withdrawing from it. Preachers are fond of reminding us of the inner connection between the big and the little responses; that if we continually say no in the small events of life we are likely to fail at the crucial moments when big issues are at stake. This is an important truth, for it underlines how our attitude to life is a continuous thing which grows or diminishes from situation to situation and can never be put in cold storage to be used when needed. Our attitude to life is after all *ourselves*, and only ceases when we cease. We cannot pretend to ourselves that deep down we are different from our everyday selves, because our everyday selves are our real selves.

It is the meaning of the gospel taught and lived by Jesus Christ that men must have the attitude of saying yes to the succeeding situations of life and never turn in on themselves. Turning in on self, saying no to life, is the attitude which is at the root of all the sins against Christ's teaching like uncharity and pride, and all the less-than-Christian responses like postponing decisions and brushing difficult knowledge away from our conscious minds. All these latter responses are forms of repression, equivalent ways of saying no to life by putting off the decision to say yes. Putting off the decision to say yes is often more harmful to the character than saying no outright, for life does not wait for us. If we are not going forward to meet each situation creatively, we are going backwards. There is either growth or diminishment, no third option.

In the second place we are asked to say yes to people. Saying yes to life more often than not involves saying yes to people. Let us be clear that, by saying yes to people, we do not mean cultivating the attitude of the yes man. We mean rather an attitude of affirmative, co-operative engagement towards our fellow men and women in the situations that bring them into our life. This means saying yes to people in the way that, for instance, a telephone samaritan says yes to the anonymous caller, knowing that the initial 'yes, come round straight away' will lead to a series of unforeseeable further yeses which will cost all the time, trouble, anxiety and loss of independence that becoming involved in another human being inevitably brings. Saying yes in this way is clearly not being a yes man in the colloquial sense of the term, for the yes man is in fact one who says no to life under the guise of saying yes, one who chooses the easy option because it is less trouble. In the true sense, saying yes to people means entering into an engagement with them, relating to them positively and creatively, being willing to share time and privacy with them – in which sharing there may often be occasions when we have to say no in order to remain helpful and creative towards them. It is always possible to turn away from people who intrude into our lives and this refusal to be affirmative is often disguised. Professed Christians seldom explicitly exclude people from their love, for that would be too obviously un-Christian, but there are any number of equivalent ways we have of saying no, e.g. passing by on the other side of the road because we are too busy to stop. There is no space to go into all these negative reactions. It would be the subject of a paper on its own. Suffice to note, therefore, that we refuse help to people in two ways: consciously and explicitly by saying we are not going to help – sins of uncharity, laziness, carelessness, malice, selfishness and so on; unconsciously and implicitly by accepting without question all the built-in barriers to social and personal life which our less-than-Christian society creates. These barriers are the barriers of class, creed, race, colour, even politics, with which our individual lives are fenced around. They in turn are thrown up by the deep-seated urge in man to remain alone and apart within a controllable community and not be drawn into relations with 'outsiders'. How many Christians living in this country passively accept these fences as given and do nothing to abolish them, settling for living their Christian lives within barriers laid down by the *status quo* rather than making their Christian lives precisely the breaking through and down of these barriers? Saying yes to people means breaking through these barriers, having the unwashed and smelly into our houses, allowing coloured men to meet our daughters, being seen as a priest with scandalous people, overcoming our native shyness and inhibitions which are so often consecrated by society instead of being uprooted. It is easy to talk about this in the abstract, but I think all of us will have to admit that we find it as difficult to combat these unconscious obstacles to Christian love which are in us as to combat the conscious ones like laziness and malice.

By the way we handle our relationships with people we either grow or diminish in personality. 'Through the Thou a man becomes I' (Buber). This means, for everybody, accepting the challenge of breaking out of the shell in which we are born and develop, with its conscious and unconscious layers noted above. There can be no growth without some breaking out; sooner or later for everyone there is the decision to say yes and to leave behind the security of past patterns and walk out into the unknown. Not to do so when the moment comes is to say no to life and people, and so diminish. Rosemary Haughton in her books has written cogently on the need for this transformation and the vital part played by passion in it; passion may be seen as the God-given catalyst which allows the transformation to take place. Without it, the necessary energy would be lacking for this bold action. The result of this act is the achievement of 'personal' living, that is life lived truly authentically, no longer according to patterns laid down by teaching from outside, or behind masks thrown up by ourselves for our protection and inner security, but from within, from the centre of our true, unmasked self. It means meeting people and treating them as people in their own right and no longer as 'opponents' or threats to oneself. It means, in other words, loving them and centring upon them away from self.

In the third place we are asked to say yes to society. For long we have been giving assent to the truth that man is a social being with duties to society, but it is especially in this generation that Catholics in this country are being led to realize that a Christian commitment to society means not only trying to live an individually Christian life in secular society but trying to make that society Christian.

It is one thing, and an important one, to aim at personal Christianity and to sanctify one's relations with other people, as we have been noting. But, because of this very need for commitment to society itself, that is not enough. This means relating to society politically and doing so in a Christian way. It means being politically Christian. Here, clearly, this does not necessarily mean participating in what goes on in the House of Commons. What is meant is that because Christianity is social, and therefore salvation in part political, the real Christian must say yes to being socially and politically committed. He cannot opt out of influencing the way society is formed and governed, least of all in a democracy.

Ultimately the social principles of Christianity are aiming at unity throughout the world. Jesus died to 'gather into one the children of God who are scattered abroad' (John 11:52). Both in the worldwide field and in the society we live in, therefore, we have to aim at breaking down all those barriers which militate against unity among men, the barriers of class, creed, race, colour being the most obvious. Being a good Christian, for instance, does not mean accepting the class system of this country with its less than Christian separation of people into privileged and unprivileged, and trying to be Christian within it. It means doing one's best to abolish privileges which are based on birth or unearned wealth. As Harvey Cox noted in a different context, the coloured people imprisoned in the ghettos of American cities do not ask for friendly gaolors to ameliorate life in the slums by running youth clubs and social services, but for liberation from those slums. Saying yes to society means a Christian change of heart, but a change of heart which issues forth in Christian social action, not just in personal adjustment to a less than Christian system. To tolerate an unjust society in any way is to nullify personal spirituality. Saying yes to people must be accompanied by saying yes to society, if it is not to become an ivory tower occupation. This is what I meant when I said at the beginning that the Christian task was a threefold commitment, not three commitments. We cannot choose between saying yes to life, people or society, because saying yes to one implies saying yes to the others. There is a profound unity in human living, which only the analytical, limited mind of man divides into separate compartments. In reality we say yes or no to the whole of human living every time we react to a particular situation.

Christian life as prayer

When we say yes to life, people and society, who are we ultimately saying yes to? It is the Christian revelation that the answer to that question is God. Christ came to tell us that the fundamental reality of our lives, the ultimate ground of our existence, in which we live and move and have our being, is the Father. Behind all the events of our lives, watching over us, caring for us, counting the number of hairs on our head, knowing when a sparrow falls to the ground, is the loving concern of the Father. God is not a remote being, far away and separate from this world, who knows us from an infinite distance, but is the very energy we live by, a divine field of force in which we operate, which is at the same time supremely personal and, according to Jesus, fatherly. This means that the events of life, our meetings with people, the social situations we find ourselves in, are watched and planned and sent by God who permeates our history from within, so that we could call everything that happens to us the fringe of his garment which we either reach out to touch or hold back from. Teilhard called matter the 'Jacob's Ladder' by which we

71

mount up to heaven, and an earlier Jesuit called the events of our lives sacraments of the present moment. It is the same insight, the realization that God is present within our lives, and therefore the responses we make to the challenge of life are personal responses to God. There is no escaping from him or exiling him innocuously to heaven. Each event of life is his clear call to us, personal and urgent, here and now.

It becomes clear that for the Christian the threefold commitment of life is fundamentally a commitment to God. This means in the first place that life can be made into a prayer and in the second place that the whole of life can be a prayer. Life can be made into a prayer. How? By simply realizing that when we say yes to life, people and society, we are deep down also saying yes to God, or rather not *also* saying yes as if God were still separate from the events of life, but saying yes to God within the events of life. Thus getting out of bed in the morning is not just facing life (whatever 'life' is) but facing God, and opening difficult letters courageously is facing the Father whose providence knows about the letter and into whose mysterious plan it falls. Even more, our relationships to people, both the ones who excite and please us and the ones we find it difficult to love, are relationships to God. We have Christ's graphic word for this in his description of the Judgement, so that there is now no excuse for us to say but *when* did we see you as a coloured immigrant or as a down-and-out and not bother about you, Lord? Likewise our political action for the betterment of society is also an encounter with God, not only in the sense that God is in society but also in the sense that he is in *us*, and our actions within the secular world are joint actions with him for the progress of humanity. The signs of the kingdom in Christ's day were the healing of the sick, the liberating of the imprisoned and the preaching of the good news to poor people, and these signs should still be present in our day through our efforts. By participating in this continuing redeeming activity of Christ in society and making it happen, the Christian ensures that the signs of the kingdom are still in this world. Such Christian action in the secular world is prayer, for it is saying yes to God's will for society, and making it come about. This is a creative yes which brings about an event like our Lady's fiat at the Annunciation, and ensures that it is not a passive yes which merely submits to events as beyond control.

Seen in this way, life not only becomes a prayer, but the whole of life becomes a prayer. There is now no action which cannot be made into a prayer, because God is present in every corner of man's life. Man's commitment to himself, to other people and to society is never-ending, has no gaps. It follows, then, that man's commitment to God Who is the divine reality undergirding his life, other people and society, is also never-ending and has no gaps. This is no new truth. It is found in the New Testament with St Paul's injunction to pray without ceasing, and was part of the Jewish consciousness of the closeness of Yahweh to his Chosen People – like the bridal dress round the bride, said Jeremiah. The point is to make these encounters real meetings with God, and not just give lip service to the theoretical truth. It is, after all, one thing to talk about the presence of God everywhere in the sacrament of the present moment, but quite another to live as if this astonishing thing were true. The witness God asks of us, most especially in the modern world, is the witness of actions not just of words. Words cost little when they are spoken from the rostrum and are unaccompanied by deeds. The Christian word has always been meant to be an event as well as a sound from the mouth.

Christian prayer

Perhaps you are thinking that the line I am adopting on prayer is to deny that it is valid as a separate act and to hold that the only prayer for a Christian committed to living in the world is the prayer of his life. At this point, therefore, I would like to dissociate myself from that view, which I regard as naive and superficial. It is naive because it ignores the plain reality of human love, and it is superficial in a Christian because it ignores the example and precept of Jesus in the gospels. By grace we are raised to the ineffable privilege of being adopted into the family of God, of becoming as it were honorary members of the Blessed Trinity. These are perhaps flippant words to use about the reality of our adoption in grace, but the theologians are clear that what happens to us at baptism is our adoption by God the Father so that by grace we can call ourselves brothers and co-heirs of his kingdom with Jesus and live the new life of grace by the Spirit of God. There is even the tradition in the Church that by grace we are *divinized*, made as it were members of the Godhead. In whatever way these mysteries are explained, theology and revelation make it apparent that by grace man is enabled to relate personally to God so that his whole life is capable of becoming a personal relationship to the Father through the Son in the Spirit. Father Alfaro describes grace as 'a permanent disposition which capacitates man for an I–Thou relationship with God, and is manifested in the personal communication of faith, hope and charity'.* If this is so, it should be plain that grace enables a man to enter into the deepest possible kind of human relationship with God, one that is equal to and even surpasses the relationships he has with his fellow men. The love a man

* From Juan Alfaro, *Persona y Gracia*, Gregorianum, vol. 41, pp. 5–29.

is enabled to have for God may indeed be dependent in this life on faith and conducted in hope and therefore at times be dim and bleak, but the Bible is sure that it is a deep and lasting union similar to the other deep and lasting unions we have in this world, wife with husband, son with father, child with mother. In other words grace enables us to *love* God. That being so, it does not do justice to the biblical and theological truth to regard the Christian life as one merely of joint work and action with God. That is not how love is expressed by man. Love may indeed make two human beings work for each other and be the base from which they work together for other people, but the essence of it is that they enjoy each other's company and relate to each other. They have expressed their love in mutual service but it is itself something deeper. The marriage where the wife was too busy looking after the needs of her husband to talk with him or give herself to him would not be a true love match. In fact one comes across such marriages and discovers that the frantic busyness of both the spouses for each other's well-being is often an escape from a deeper meeting between each other which they are too scared to risk. The essence of the I–Thou relationship is the spending of time together, the *wasting* of time from a utilitarian point of view, for love is essentially daft. It is the same between the 'graced' Christian and God. Each wants the person of the other, not just a mutual service or joint participation in action. The tradition of twenty centuries of Christianity has in fact borne this out, for in every age the deepest Christian relationship has been seen to be that of prayer. In more recent times the Dutch Catechism has expressed this tradition thus:

To try to live well – is that prayer enough? It is already a great deal. And some people do in fact restrict them-

selves to this. A day of demanding duties leaves them
with little peace. They manage no more than a prayer
which they find fleeting and unreal. Then they find it
more in keeping with God's infinite mystery to let their
ordinary life itself be their answer. This is at least honest.
But is it fully human? And is it possible in the long run?
Is it human to be always silent where we really care for
someone? And is it possible to persevere thus in faith
and obedience? At the most difficult moment of his life
Jesus gave the warning: 'Watch and pray that you may
not enter into temptation; the spirit indeed is willing but
the flesh is weak' (Matt. 26:41). We cannot do without
watchfulness. Otherwise obedience will deteriorate into
self will. The sense of the presence of God will vanish,
and at the moment of trial we will forget his will and
disregard it. There can be no work without contem-
plation, no expansion without exploration in depth. Love
cannot exist without self-expression (pp. 311–12).

When we turn to the New Testament we see that Jesus
manifested this truth in his relationship with the Father.
He both practised prayer himself by spending nights at it
in between his busy, totally available days, and he taught
his disciples to pray. Significantly it was after he had spent
a night alone in prayer that his followers came to him and
said, 'Lord teach *us* to pray.' The Lord's Prayer was given
to men by a man who had just come down from the hills
after a whole night of prayer. To interpret it merely in
terms of Christian action is surely to miss the essence of
the son to father relationship which it is meant to express.

Prayer is saying yes to God. This links it up with life,
for we have seen that the Christian life is precisely that –
saying yes to God who is hidden in the centre of every
event. So prayer may be seen as a moment of focus for the

76

whole of our life, a moment when we make explicit and articulate the implicit direction of our lives. Our whole lives are saying yes to God, in people and society, but we need to make this explicit, to say it directly to the Father. When we stay still for a moment and pray, we turn directly to God and give him our whole lives. Thus prayer is not an operation in the gaps of life which we have to stop living to perform, or turn aside from our commitments to do. It is the focusing of our attention upon God so that we can give ourselves, commitments and all, to him more meaningfully. We never live more fully as Christians than when we turn the whole direction of our lives towards God and give them totally to him. Doing this is not escaping from life into a side issue but charging our life with renewed energy and zeal. It is the central act of that life of faith, hope and charity which grace enables us to live. By saying yes to God explicitly in prayer we ensure that the life from the centre of which this cry has gone up is itself a steady yes to life, people and society. Without that explicit moment of prayer there is a real danger that the lives of Christians in this world may be only theoretically lived as prayer. In practice you can only pray all the time everywhere if you bother to pray some of the time somewhere. There is a risk of hypocrisy in the man who says his whole life is a prayer and leaves it at that. One often wonders if he knows what he is saying. My experience is that the people who really do make their life a prayer and seem to work without stop for and with God are the ones who spend a considerable time on their knees in explicit prayer. So far from providing them with an escape from other people, the face to face encounter with the living God which prayer is has forced them out of themselves to love other men in a way that the more leisured approach of those who 'pray their whole life' does not evince. The latter seem not to have encountered the awesome and demanding mystery of God for all that their lives are busy in his service.

The relationship, then, between the total Christian life and prayer may be summed up by saying that the latter is the expression and the source of the former. Prayer is first of all the *expression* of Christian commitment. It is the making explicit of the implicit yes to God which a zealous Christian life is. In the course of our lives we exhibit a hundred different faces and identities to people, being now sympathetic, now justly angry, now the leader, now the led; now narrow and rigid, now broad and tolerant. In our everyday commutations from home to work to recreation we assume a vast number of identities. Which identity, which face, is our real one? The answer is an amalgam of them all, for none of them is false, though none of them is the whole self. It is precisely in prayer to God that this amalgam comes together in a recognizable whole. The face we turn to God is the face of the whole of our life, the total identity gathered from the changing episodes of our life. In prayer everything in us 'comes together' and is presented to God. That is why, among other things, prayer is a psychologically helpful operation, for it serves to integrate us. You can hide things from people and even from yourself by only showing selected facets of your character in public. Genuine prayer prevents that because nothing can be hidden from God. He sees all. The whole man, every nook and corner of his personality, is exposed in prayer. The face we turn to God is our real face. *That* is our identity. The poet draws the ultimate theological message out of this when he remarks that the just man achieves his identity by being more than merely himself, for he

Acts in God's eye what in God's eye he is –
Christ – for Christ plays in ten thousand places,

78

Lovely in limbs, and lovely in eyes not his
To the Father through the features of men's faces.*

Prayer is secondly the *source* of our Christian life of love. I do not think it necessary to expand this particular truth, because it is one of the best known of Christian themes. From Jesus onwards preachers have urged us to watch and pray, adore and love, so that our prayers may bear fruit in loving lives. I would, however, draw attention in particular to the necessity of prayer as a source of theological knowledge. Only by prayer, it seems to me, can we learn to let our knowledge *about* God pass over into a knowledge *of* God. They are not the same. Not all those who study and write about God show that they know him. And yet theology proper is this latter knowledge, that *sapida scientia* of the great theologians, where the intricacies of analysis and argument are seen to be part of a higher synthesis, the personal knowledge of the Father and the Son and his redemptive plan. It is this living, personal knowledge which is genuine theology, and it is also eternal life according to Jesus in John 17:3. In one of his best editorials in the *Clergy Review* Charles Davis made a plea for personal holiness in every reformer in the Church, pointing out that people today in the Church are proving not to be satisfied with new ideas because ultimately they are hungry not for change as such but for God, a hunger which only holiness in the reformers can feed. Those engaged in *aggiornamento* in the Church must, in other words, know God as well as know about him. Davis continued with a paragraph which can serve as a summary of the place of prayer in the Christian life.

Holiness demands a communing with God in personal,

* From G. M. Hopkins, 'As Kingfishers Catch Fire'.

private prayer. One may deplore the self-deception that uses prayer as a substitute for Christian action, and does this particularly when such action makes uncomfortable demands. One may react against a false spirituality that denies the sanctifying power of external action. One may insist that public worship and private devotions should not be confused. It remains true that no one can be in close personal union with God without frequent withdrawal for intimate converse with him. Part of the priestly life is to be regularly alone with God, so that one goes out to men from the depths of communion with him. (*Clergy Review*, October 1966)

Liturgy and private prayer

It should now be possible to sketch the relationship between liturgy and private prayer. All that I have been saying about prayer could be said about liturgical prayer as well as private prayer. Both liturgy and private prayer are an explicit yes to God from the centre of life, and both liturgy and private prayer are the expression and the source of Christian life. The difference lies in what they express and what they are the source of. As regards the source, I should say that while both private prayer and liturgy can be said to be the source of further Christian action on the part of those who engage in them, liturgy can in addition be said to be itself the source of private prayer. Liturgy is the worship of the Body of Christ, the official prayer of Christian life. Through liturgy the individual Christian is linked and re-linked constantly with Christ. From baptism onwards the source of his life in Christ is liturgical action. Above all in the Eucharist he is fed on Christ and linked with the Body of the Church. Thus his very Christian life finds its source in the liturgy. Part of this Christian life, as we have seen, is private prayer. Clearly, then, private prayer finds its source in liturgy. It is in fact a continuation in private of the public acts of the liturgy, as it were a 'holding' of the supreme moments of the mass and sacraments. The moment of communion or the moment of the great doxology at the end of the canon of the mass are over all too quickly. The fervent Christian will want to prolong those moments in the secrecy of his heart. He does this in private prayer. It is the same with the other sacraments. Every prayer of sorrow for sin is a renewal of the sacrament of penance, every prayer for health a preparation for or return to the sacrament of the sick in which Christ comes to heal our diseases. Private prayer, then, is a continuation in secret of the public, communal acts of the liturgy.

As regards prayer being the expression of Christian life, the relationship between liturgy and private prayer is that liturgy can be said to be the expression of the Christian yes to life, people and society made by the Church gathered for that purpose, while private prayer is the expression of that threefold yes made by each individual person who makes up the people of God. We saw above that Christian living involves an affirmative, creative response to people and society, and that ultimately this response was made to God hidden in the depths of both people in particular and society in general. We then saw that prayer was the explicit affirmation of this yes. Clearly, in view of the subtle interplay of communal and individual responses in the Christian life, there is need for this explicit yes to be made both in a public act and a private act. The public act is the liturgy. The private act is prayer. In liturgy we, the Church, stand before God in Christ and say yes to life, people and society; and then in prayer we repeat this affirmation in the privacy of our hearts. The affirmative response to God's call has to be made simultaneously by the Church, the people of

God gathered to answer God, and by each individual member of that assembly so as to prevent the communal response being merely an empty show. There is, of course, a reciprocity between the two, each act feeding and supporting the other.

I think we can go further in our comparison and say that in practice liturgy is primarily concerned with the response men and women make to people and society, with the response to life presupposed and in the background, while in private prayer it is the fundamental yes to life which is predominant, with the yes to people and society in the background. Clearly the response made to people and society is especially focused in the liturgy because it is there that people and society are to be found. Liturgy is all about communal living. It is a holy communion, communion between God and the people in one great affirmative amen.

In so far as the distinction we made between a man or woman relating to people and relating to society is valid, we then get two kinds of liturgy. Liturgy as the expression of the former is the liturgy of house masses and informal groups. Liturgy as the expression of the latter is the formal liturgy of the parish church. There is room for both, since both kinds of assembly are natural to man. There is first of all the informal gathering of primary groups, get-togethers of people who have established a fairly intimate relationship and share a common interest such as their profession or the place they live in. The liturgy that is appropriate for this sort of group is the informal mass round the table with spontaneity the dominant element. It is good to know that this kind of liturgy is growing in the Church, as groups of parishioners gather to study the Bible or Vatican Council decrees, or to form Catholic Family Movement groups. In this category, too, can be placed the masses for specialist groups like 'red masses' for lawyers, masses for teachers and nurses, and especially masses in schools for children. In this primary group liturgy I think it unwise for the authorities to legislate rubrically, because the very nature of the gathering points towards spontaneity. Instead they should encourage experiment and freedom, and risk having the odd unseemly event, which is probably no more shocking than the attempt to observe rubrics made for large basilicas in small family rooms.

Secondly there is the formal secondary group, which for Christians is above all the parish. Here the relationship is not intimate and it is unwise to expect it to be so. By its nature it is a coming together of men and women of very different types and backgrounds, tastes and language. One has only to think of the average city parish Sunday mass to realize that this gathering is not and cannot be an intimate, informal one. Nevertheless, it is a vastly important gathering, because it is the expression of the Christian duty to break down barriers and create unity by social action. As we saw, living the Christian life means not only living a personally loving life within the confines set up for oneself by society, but also christianizing that society by trying to break down the barriers. The parish liturgy, public and not intimate, is the expression of this communal Christian task. As such it is *the* Christian liturgical act, because Christianity is not a religion for a select coterie of like-minded people, but a gathering of all people into the one Church. I agree that there is a place for a liturgy to express intimate gatherings, but such liturgy is only secondary to the main purpose of the mass and the sacraments, which is to unite all people whether they like each other or not, have the same occupations and tastes or not, in the one Body of Christ. Because the Church is the Church and not a sect, public liturgy, with the full observance of the rubrics and proper formality, is the supreme expression of the Church's worship. It is the most important yes of the week.

Before and beneath our Christian yes to people and to society is our original yes to life. From this fundamental attitude, typified for me by getting up in the morning, springs our attitude to the people we meet and the society we belong to. Will our attitude be creative and co-operative, or will it be negative and escapist? It depends deep down on our attitude to life – do we say yes or no to that? This fundamental attitude to life is best cultivated in private prayer. It needs articulating, and it is done by prayer, when we stand before God, in Christ, and give ourselves wholly to him. I would like to make a plea for a stretching to the limits in this area of Christian commitment. Christ spent nights in prayer. There is surely a need for his followers to imitate him in this by organizing vigils and fasts, or at any rate setting aside generous portions of time for spending in the Father's company. In this way our lives will grow towards God, not only in prayer but in the other times too, precisely because our reaching out to God in prayer will have the effect of making us find him everywhere. It is of course notoriously difficult to find time to pray in our busy lives, but I do not think that the fact of it being difficult absolves us from the need to do it. That is not how love works. Where there is the will there must be the way. To help us solve the difficulty perhaps we should begin to plan our lives in terms of the weekly cycle rather than the daily cycle. Each day it is difficult for ordinary Christians to give more than a few minutes to prayer, but could they not find an hour for prayer each week? An hour of private prayer once a week might well prove possible for a layman and be an invaluable element in his Christ life. Meanwhile for priests I think such an hour is not impossible every day.

The last point I would like to make is to emphasize the fact that all prayer, liturgical or private, is towards Mystery. In this it is like life and love. Growing acquaintance with any person or job has the paradoxical effect of making us realize that we know less rather than more about what we are doing and who we are loving. It is in fact not the stranger who is a mystery to me but my deepest friend. The more I associate with him and grow deep in my love for him the more I come to see that in the heart of every human being is an area of incommunicability which is opaque to me and which I can never enter or possess. It is the secret of successful friendship, as of successful marriage, to recognize this. If, then, the I-Thou relationship between two human beings is a growth towards mystery, how much more will the Christ life, in which we finite humans grow towards the infinite God, be also a mystery. I mention this as a postscript to my paper because I am convinced that what we need to remember today in this exciting time of change and discovery in Christian living is the ineffable element in prayer. No human being can ever imagine, conceive or circumscribe God in any way with his mind. Before the Godhead we are destined to remain speechless in a cloud of unknowing. We must remember this in all the discussion about the models for God and prayer which are being tried today. Of course we need new models for the approach to God, models which speak to men today and have some relevance for modern man 'come of age'. But in the last analysis we must remember that all human models of God are infinitely inadequate, whether they are old fashioned ones which picture a God out there or up-to-date ones which speak of a divine field of force and ground of our being. The discussion of new images for God and his revelation is important as a matter of communication between Christians and their contemporaries within and without the Church, and I would not like to give the impression that I regard the debate about God as unimportant. But it is essentially a debate about apologetics – getting the truth across to people – not about prayer, which is reaching out to God. For this latter action we do not need models except at the beginning of our quest. The moment of truth is the moment when we realize that our images are a hindrance to our pursuit and then have the courage to jettison them. That is the moment we enter into the Mystery, now no longer merely conceptually grasped but lived existentially with our whole selves. When that happens the surface tensions between Christian life and Christian prayer, and between liturgical and private prayer, dissolve and give way to a new unity, in which the apparent oppositions now no longer count because they are seen to be merely different paths towards a summit where all paths meet. On that summit is the presence of God. It is where we should be too, as long as we remember that its location is the centre of this world.

7

Some Reflections on Spiritual Direction for Priests

One of the points that St Thérèse of Lisieux used to make was that she had little time for complicated methods of spiritual direction and relied on the fact that Jesus himself was her spiritual director who always gave her the correct guidance when she called upon him. On the face of it this remark is beguilingly simple and could be taken as advice to have no spiritual director, but if you look at the practice of Thérèse you will see that in fact she often asked for and received spiritual advice and can be seen to have had directors. What she reacted against in this, as in all departments of spirituality, was an excessive complication of method which she knew obscured the simple demands of the gospel and took people's eye off Jesus Christ by making them look at themselves too much. I think that, as so often, Thérèse proves as sound a guide for the end of the twentieth century as she was for the end of the nineteenth. We priests need to have spiritual direction but God preserve us from a complicated methodology which will take us away from the simplicity and also the stark demands of the gospel.

Priorities in work

Even after thirty years I can still be puzzled by the bewildering variety of duties that lie ahead of me every day in the parish. Every day after breakfast, I am faced with a crowd of possible things to do. I am free to do any, or none, of them. There is probably little danger that I will do none of them, but there is considerable danger that I will gird myself up to do the 'wrong' ones and spend much energy in the wrong direction which could have been spent better if I had stopped to work out priorities. Stopping to look at one's priorities is an important part of the stewardship of one's time and talents. One of the tags I remember from the army is 'Time spent in reconnaissance is never wasted'. To reconnoitre the ground, then, is never a waste of time. There is plenty of ground! What follows is my own particular view. Priest readers will be able to make their own additions or subtractions as they read. I give the list in no particular order, because that is precisely the problem: there *is* no order.

I should be generous in putting my energies into working with my fellow priests in the parish and, if there is a team, in helping to make the parish team a united group. In this, good will is not enough. One has to spend time with one's pastor or assistants. I must not become the sort of priest who is 'marvellous' with parishioners but difficult to live with, impossible to work with.

I should be generous in visiting parishioners in their homes, because there is no alternative way of knowing them and letting them know me as pastor. But a problem arises. Should I concentrate on the elderly, or the sick, or married couples struggling, or lonely single people, or young people? There will be voices raised for each of those categories, voices which are often passionately critical if I am considered to be neglecting a particular group.

I should visit the sick in hospital, and, if there is a hospital in the parish care, I must never fail in my duties there both by day visiting and answering emergencies at night.

I should be careful to keep in touch with the parish primary school. Teachers and pupils feel neglected by a priest who leaves them to get on with things without him. Adult formation is, surely, far more important than school work. This requires much looking for leaders, training them, evenings spent in group work, personal preparation as resource person for lay leaders.

I should be intelligent and generous in introducing a sacramental programme into the parish. Nearly every one of the sacraments requires a 'course' of some sort: involving parents, teachers, the priest. Marriage, especially, requires the setting up of a necessarily rather elaborate course of preparation for the engaged couples.

I should prepare my sermons assiduously. I must not let the multitudinous tasks which absorb my energy as pastor make me careless and empty as a preacher. This means having the ability to step aside from being caught up in what is happening in order to preach and prophesy about what might be happening. The frankly utopian should have a part in my thinking and planning. Parishes get nowhere without vision in the clergy.

I should also prepare liturgy well. Gone are the days when you could arrive vested in the sanctuary and read it all from the book. Today a priest is required to have spent time with musicians, readers, planners in order to produce a live liturgy. Parish liturgy is, among other things, the shop-window of the parish. People can be turned off or on surprisingly deeply by the parish mass on Sunday.

I should be careful not to confine my energies to the sometimes soft option of the sacristy and sanctuary, but become involved in the local community as a means of involving the parishioners in it. This often takes a lot of time, much of it spent in boring meetings. What the French call 'presence' can be very costing.

I should read the Bible endlessly, engaging in daily *lectio divina* in order to become a man of the Bible, thoroughly penetrated by the Word of God.

I should study theology because that is the science of my profession. If I do not open a book of theology from year to year I am neglecting my 'patients' as much as a doctor who does not keep up to date with medical progress. Theology is best studied by going on courses and taking theological journals. It is not enough simply to re-read old works.

I should take time off, visit my family and friends, learn to relax, take physical exercise, have some cultural pursuits, read books other than professional ones.

I should set aside time for personal prayer, the prolonged communion with God which no disciple can afford to neglect, without which all the above activities may become empty and uninspiring, because not grounded in God, the centre of my being.

Finally, amidst all these activities I should be available to the call of the telephone and the doorbell and not say 'no' to those who come (in increasing numbers in our society) for help and guidance. The person who calls is Christ, and I must never be too busy to give time to him or her, be he in the disguise of down-and-out looking for help, distracted client sent by the Samaritans, or fellow priest getting away from the pressures of his own parish to spend time with another priest.

Guidance

Clearly there is a need to be constantly checking one's priorities as a priest in a parish and to have some sort of strategy worked out. If one does not make oneself aware of the whole field of duties calling to be performed, one runs the risk of having no plan and ending up simply as a reactor to events regardless of priorities. That is, to say the least, careless and lacking in responsibility.

This is where it is good to have another person to talk things over with. An objective other party, who knows me well, will best help me to sort out my priorities and prevent me choosing only the congenial tasks and conveniently forgetting about the less congenial ones on the grounds that I have no time for them. The phrase 'I have no time to. . .' is one that priests should be wary of. It so often means 'I have no inclination to . . .' In other words it is a more or less conscious rationalization. The real reason, if I am honest, that I avoid, say, parish visiting is that I find it tiresome or difficult. However, I do not like to admit this even to myself, so I say I have no time for it. This is generally dishonest. We nearly always have time for the things we want to do. Therefore, in drawing up with a candid friend a list of priorities of work, it is often helpful to draw up also a list of the things which I like doing and, alongside it, a list of the things I do not like doing. This double list will help me to be honest when I come to assessing what is the order of priorities in my priestly work. In this exercise the candid friend is helping me to know myself and my hidden desires and choices in order to work more effectively for God. The candid friend is helping me towards self-knowledge, so is already becoming a spiritual director to me.

Self knowledge

We all need self-knowledge, but those who work with people (like doctors, social workers, personnel managers) need it more than anyone. To begin with we ought to know our good points and our bad points, the datum of our persons, so as to be able to make allowances for our weaknesses and to capitalize on our talents. If I have a talent for imaginative planning but none for day-to-day management, I ought to know and remember that. It will help me to be patient with those who have no imagination (through no fault of their own). It will also help me to be patient with myself over my routine inefficiency and be humble enough to ask for help. What a lot of unnecessary distress can be prevented in a parish by priests and leaders who know their own strengths and weaknesses and are humble enough to do something with that knowledge!

As well as knowing our conscious gifts and lacks, we should also be on the way to knowing our unconscious selves. Our unconscious self is our temperament. We cannot change it. It is given to us by life. But to know and accept it certainly helps us live and work with it. It is good for all priests to know whether they are introverted or extroverted; intuitive or going by evidence; swayed by thinking things out or by feeling towards a solution; given to elaborate planning or inspired reaction at the moment of decision. We are all differently constituted in these departments, as the Myers-Briggs Type Indicator reveals. No one temperament is better than another. Each person is uniquely gifted. But when I know my temperament to be what it is, then I am much more capable of making objective judgements about people and situations than if I am ignorant of myself. It is like the game of bowls. You have to know the exact bias in your bowl if you are to have any chance of getting near the jack. You 'aim off' accordingly. One's judgements of people and situations in a parish require that sort of knowledge of oneself and one's biases. Then you can 'aim off' correctly and achieve objectivity.

A spiritual director can help us to know ourselves, chiefly

because he or she is a third party. No one can know self by oneself. It requires that third party.

A healthy relationship with a spiritual guide can then go deeper and proceed to help us sort out the deeper motivations of our life. Most of us have jealousies and envies which cloud our judgements and make our actions less than Christian. We have hidden drives both sexually and towards power. The celibate especially needs to come to terms with these drives in an atmosphere of honest appraisal so as to prevent disastrous 'explosions'. A certain priest after many years of relatively tranquil heterosexual chastity suddenly found himself landed with a homosexual passion for a man twenty years younger than himself. He talked it over with a priest friend who helped him not to be ashamed of it and to live with it blamelessly and with a light humorous touch. The priest friend by his patience and acceptance defused a potentially disastrous situation and helped a naturally melancholic man out of much bewilderment and pain.

Finally we should all know and acknowledge our hidden fears and insecurities. These especially make us difficult to live with and ineffective in our pastoral work, because of the artificial barriers we erect through unacknowledged fear. These barriers hide our true self from our parishioners, make us awkward and abrupt in dealing with people, make us run away from the people who need us most. Simply because they have not faced up to their hidden insecurities, some priests hide from situations which may cause them hurt, or bluster their way out of such situations, and so cause unnecessary hurt to others. Here again a candid spiritual friend who knows me well and whom I can trust can help me enormously here. He will not remove my fears, but he can get me to accept them without the need for masks and hostility to others. He can pray with me *through* them and so disarm their destructiveness on self and others. Firm compassion from a spiritual director can help me grow through my weaknesses and make them instruments of growth. That, surely, is the heart of the gospel of Jesus Christ. 'When I am weak then I am strong'. But we have to know our weaknesses first before we can allow grace to turn it into strength.

To know God

Here I have examined the role of spiritual director from the outside in. First he is useful to help a priest work out his priorities at the comparatively superficial level of parish work. This leads into the realm of self-knowledge where all agree that spiritual direction is a necessity. The final layer, the deepest area of self, is where we meet God, know and are known by him, sink and merge into him as the Ground of our being. This deep area exists in us all. It is where we are united to God in being and in activity. It is the source of all activity, the living spring of our personalities. How reluctant we sometimes are to visit this area!

The priest, other Christ, steward of God's mysteries, ministers of his Word and sacraments should especially be conversant with this deep area in himself. He should be able to go there without fear, meet his God openly and courageously in the depth of his being. He should, in fact, be an expert in this deep encounter area. If he avoids it, he is but a shallow operator on the surface of things. Priests who, in humility, know about the depths of human personality by prayer, draw many to them for guidance. They are healers in our society.

My conviction is that we all need a spiritual guide to go with us on this inward journey. It is unwise to go it alone, without the advice and companionship of one who has been there himself. Hence the need for priests to have a spiritual friend with whom we can share the deepest things, and under whose guidance we may find our soul. When we have found our soul we can live fruitfully the ever present tension caused by our high ideals (received from the gospel) and our distressingly low performance over the years. United in God in the depth of our being we can not only survive this tension but make it an instrument of our priestly work. We can live happily though the muddle caused by all those conflicting duties mentioned at the beginning of this article. In my experience they are frequently a source of anxiety at the surface level tempting me to quit trying to sort them all out, but never a worry at the deep level, where God meets me and I meet God. At that level all is grace and sheer thanksgiving; in fact all is joy.

8

Light and Salt: an Experience of Priesthood

The priest is called by the gospel to play many roles:
  as celebrant and communicator of the Good News to our
    modern world;
  as prophet of justice and peace in society;
  as co-ordinator and supporter of all the exciting lay
    ministries which are available in parishes today;
  as pastor who knows and is known by his flock and is
    present in the crisis situations of their lives.
But in this article I have chosen to be more personal and
to share with you an experience of priesthood to which I
seem to have been called in the thirty years since my
ordination. I have always been insistent on the need for
prayer, deep contemplative prayer, in my life and have
tried to practise it. At present I get up every morning at
6.30 and pray till 8.00, when I get myself some breakfast.
But in earlier times as a priest I have prayed for as much
as four hours a day and have seen this as necessary for me.
As a result of this prayer I have felt called to exercise my
priesthood in a certain way, which I shall now try to
outline.

There are two traditions about contemplative prayer in
the Catholic Church. One is that the deeper you want to
go into prayer the more you must be separated from the
world. This is the tradition of the enclosed monastic orders
— Carthusians, Cistercians, Carmelites, for example.

However, a second tradition also exists. It goes back to Jesus Christ's own witness, and has been revived in this century by, for instance, Charles de Foucauld and his followers. This is that the deeper you go in contemplative prayer the more you will become involved in the world. In this tradition there is no enclosure behind which prayer goes on. Rather, the prayer of the community opens us up to involvement in society, especially through hospitality. I have found myself called in prayer to follow this second tradition, for I have discovered that the barriers between my own ego and God which have to be broken down in prayer prove to be the very same barriers that exist between me and other people. The painful process of sharing my privacy with the Lord in prayer and allowing him into my life is the same process by which I share with other human beings. There are not two sets of barriers but only one, and prayer is the crucial activity which melts it. If I were asked for a word which sums up this process of 'letting God in' in prayer and life, I would choose 'sharing'. Sharing is a two-way process. I share my life with Christ either through serving him in my neighbour or directly in prayer; but I only do so because he has already shared his life with me in the incarnation and in the daily event of grace. Grace is a two-way flow from God to me in Christ; from me back to God in Christ. Sharing is the key to it.

In the Sermon on the Mount, Our Lord used two striking metaphors of sharing to illustrate how his followers were to spread the good news of the kingdom of God. One was the metaphor of light, the other that of salt (Mat. 5:13–16). Both are examples of sharing. Light spreads itself out in the surrounding darkness, dispelling this darkness as it spreads. Salt also works by sharing itself with its surrounds, permeating the surrounding food with its sharpness. Have you noticed, however, the difference between the two as

97

well as the similarity? Light is most effective when it is
separated from its surrounds in the sense of being lifted
up. It has to be raised on high to be seen. It is of little use
unless it is elevated. If I walk into a dark room and light
a match so as to see where everything is, I automatically
raise the lighted match above my head to make its illumi-
nation go further; I do not keep it at waist level. Jesus, of
course, recognized this. Lights have to be set on lampstands
to be effective (vv. 14–15). Salt, on the other hand, works
differently. It must not be kept apart or elevated, but
must be mixed in with the surrounds so as to become
indistinguishable. I put salt in the soup and stir it around
so that it gets lost; if it were to stay in a lump in one corner
of the soup it would not be doing its job.

Applying Christ's two metaphors to the pastoral priesthood I suggest that we should aim at being spiritually
light and socially salt. Being spiritually light means being
separated from society in terms of our values. We have to
aim at higher values than those of contemporary society.
We have to be 'above' the world in our attitude to honesty,
integrity, purity, ambition, success, what to do with money,
justice and peace. In those areas our light must shine over
the surrounding darkness. That is what we are there for:
to illuminate the darkness with the light of the gospel,
whether the darkness wants it or not. This means being
placed awkwardly and prominently on lampstands. Paradoxically we do this best in the modern world by not being
on a social pedestal, but by mixing freely and on equal
terms with everyone in society, especially poor people. This
calls for as much courage, it seems to me, as being on the
lampstand with regard to values, because it means risking
being rebuffed and misunderstood without any of the
protection afforded by a privileged position in society out
of reach of criticism. In other words we must go for being

socially salt, entirely mixed in and 'lost' in society, while vigorously maintaining our elevated position with regard to morality and values. There is no easy balance here. It is tempting to back up our separatedness in values with physical separation too (enclosure walls, forbidding presbyteries, protective housekeepers), but Jesus' metaphor is there to suggest that we must remain socially mixed in with people like salt and not withdraw to the safety of the clerically elevated pedestal, the mini-monastry of the closed priests' house.

A word about celibacy is appropriate here. It seems to me that celibacy is the perfect instrument for this work. Because we are celibate we can share the house we live in without having to think of the protection of a wife and family. Celibacy is the ideal state in life for getting more involved in more people than would be possible if we had a family household to look after. It opens up for us large possibilities of being a salty leaven in the world, able to move with freedom in society, especially in its margins. The sadness is when celibacy is combined with the monastic mentality and seen as a reason for staying behind barriers instead of being the socially liberating agent it was meant to be, as in the case of Jesus Christ and so many of the saints. If we aspire, with God's grace, to be a spiritual light to our generation, doing this by mixing freely in every corner of society with every type of person, then I can think of no better instrument for this than the Church's offer of celibacy to its ministers. I embrace that offer with gratitude.

One way for a pastoral priest to ensure that his apostolate becomes socially 'salt' is to make the house he lives in an open one where people of all kinds, catholic and non-catholic, socially acceptable and non-acceptable, can freely come without having to ring the doorbell or make an appointment. When you do this you make the house you live in itself an instrument of the apostolate. It ceases to be a rest home for tired troops behind the lines, but becomes part of the front line. University chaplains have been doing this for years with their chaplaincies. It is an understood thing, in universities, that the chaplaincy is open to students to drop in at any time of the day or night to be used as a sort of club, and chaplains have accepted this fact and built their work round it accordingly. But the idea is only beginning to catch on among the parochial clergy. It is a difficult decision to make, because it means a degree of sharing which is out of the ordinary. It means that the priest shares his life as well as his work with his parishioners. It is comparatively easy to share your work with your 'clients'. Doctors, lawyers, social workers do it all the time with devotion. But, I suggest that we priests are asked to share ourselves with our people more generously than that. After all we live beside our churches, in the midst of our parishes. We do not disappear in cars at 5 p.m. to another part of the town. We stay put, available to all who want us. The open house is merely an extension of this concept of availability which removes the last barriers of doorbell and housekeeper and so enables our availability to be genuinely extended to all who care to come. This challenge to share our lives as well as our work with the parish reminds me of a saying of St Teresa of Avila: 'We think we are giving God everything, whereas what we are really offering him is the revenue or the fruits of our land while keeping the stock and the right of ownership of it in our own hands' (*Life*, p.63). In the same way priests who want to give themselves completely to their parishioners are invited to share their lives and houses with their flocks, not keep back a private part by way of stock, and share only the fruits in hard work outside the presbytery. We must not be capitalists but communists in communicating the gospel.

The ways this works out in practice are probably as diverse as there are parishes which try to do it. Let me, however, share with you some experiences we have had in our open house where people may come by just opening the door and walking in. In practice two groups of people avail themselves of this, though interestingly the dividing line between the groups gets increasingly blurred. The first group consists of committed parishioners who use the house for meetings, or come to work in the office, or pray in a prayer group, or for a planning session on liturgy, etc. We have no parish hall, so our house has become the parish centre where all but the largest meetings automatically take place. Our personal rooms as well as the public rooms, are convenient for this. The second group of house frequenters are those who for one reason or another find it a good place to drop into just to be around and meet people and, as it were, come off the streets. Young people predominate in this group. Every night our kitchen and TV room are full of them. They play snooker at a makeshift table at the foot of the stairs; currently monopoly has become the evening craze, where would-be capitalists act out their dreams on the cardboard property market. As many of the youth are unemployed school-leavers, it is quite poignant to see them getting keen on that particular game. Unemployment among young people is a scourge of our local society. To offer shelter and 'belonging' in our home is only a beginning of what we ought to be doing for them. We try to get them jobs. Once a week we create jobs for them and pay them for two hours work about the place. It is a tiny beginning to help them towards self-respect.

A third group of guests in our house is the marginals of city life, the down-and-outs. They come, mostly at night,

101

for shelter. We never turn them away. There is a room
with blankets and pillows where they can spend the night.
Most nights it is occupied. Of course one has to be wise
here and avoid subsidizing drunkenness by allowing the
same men in every night for free, thus enabling them to
spend their social security money in the pubs. My experience is that they understand this well and I have been
amazed at the way there is honour among the Edinburgh
down-and-outs and absence of exploitation of our 'softness'.
Another group of marginals who come to us are the
mentally handicapped. There are not a few in our district.
It is fascinating to see how they home in on our house and
spend the evening in our kitchen. By definition they are
more difficult than our other guests and need some sort of
supervision. This is where the others in the house, like
the unemployed, rally round and help. In fact a good
atmosphere of sharing in the house builds up, and I find
it far from necessary to be around when all this is taking
place. I can go about my own work in the parish and leave
the house and its occupants to get on with the work of
Christian hospitality, without benefit of my presence. On
the other hand when I am at home it is important to join
in and share with all who are around. For instance I think
it is wrong to *give* a tramp a cup of tea when he calls. One
must pour two cups and share tea with him. As for the
practice of handing out sandwiches at the door, I regard
it as positively unchristian. That is not how we should
treat Christ at our door. This bare recital probably gives
no idea of what fun it is to have a home like this. There is
seldom a dull moment; sometimes we have a big crisis like
a fight in the kitchen, frequently outbursts of temperament,
caused more often than not by drink, but most of the time
there is enormous good will and fun. I would not, and
probably by now could not, change it. You will also have

guessed by now that this way of running the presbytery spells the end of the housekeeper. To this I say: Alleluia!

I have found that having an open house and sharing as much as possible with the people of the parish, trying to promote a spirit of co-responsibility for the work of God in the parish, has led us to develop a team ministry whereby lay persons of both sexes have joined the priests as resident team-members. In this way one augments the possibilities of full-time service by expanding the range of 'priests' in the parish team. This is an example of how sharing in one department (parish house) seems to lead to sharing in other departments of parish work (personnel and ministries). Light, after all, spreads in all directions from the top of the lampstand and cannot be stopped.

I began by saying how all that has developed in my life as a priest has come from prayer. Let me end on that note too. Thirty-six years ago I had no idea where prayer would lead me, but I knew, as I entered the seminary that prayer was the most important thing I had to learn about and do. Vatican II and all that was to follow from it was still in the unknown future. I am glad I started at prayer. Without it I am sure I could never have withstood the pressures on my rather conservative temperament that the decades after Vatican II were to bring. Even more depressing is the thought of all the excitement I might have missed if I had not opened up my priesthood in prayer to what the Holy Spirit had in store for me. New life has always to be preceded by deaths, and for me new life as a priest took place after what Ivan Illich has called 'the demise of the clergyman'. We have already 'buried' the housekeeper and I hope that the clerics among my readers will join in killing off her partner 'the clergyman'.

9

Shared Responsibility

Some time ago all the priests of the Archdiocese met at Craiglockhart for a day with the Cardinal to study the new code of Canon Law. When we arrived we were each given a pack of papers, containing among other things a paper from the Bishops' Conference in Scotland written by their theological commission entitled *Life in Communion*. This excellent pamphlet was a very strong plea for more communion between priests and lay people, for more 'shared responsibility' in our parishes. It recognized honestly that there was not much of this around at the moment, that we in Scotland have a long way to go before this ideal is realized. Appropriately enough this theme of 'shared responsibility' turned out to be the main message of our day together on Canon Law, as it had been at another initiative of the Cardinal's: the week for priests, held also at Craiglockhart, when we heard about the Rite for Christian Initiation of Adults from a powerful team of speakers from the USA. I have been asked for some comments on 'shared responsibility' and agreed to do so with alacrity, because I think it is an urgent matter for us all. If, in the following paragraphs, I tread on toes, please forgive me. It is done in love. I am in a hurry. I think my fellow parish priests should be too. It is now twenty years since Vatican II.

Some priests are reluctant to share knowledge about the

finances of the parish with their parishioners. You would think that that would be the first thing we would want to share in our parishes, for after all it is parish money, not our own, which is being administered. But I know of few parishes in St Andrews and Edinburgh where accounts are published and discussed. In my experience a parish council which examines the parish accounts every month shows maturity of judgement about spending and an understanding of the diocesan regulations about money when they are explained to them, which I frankly marvel at, and which proves invaluable – a really helpful case of shared responsibility.

Some priests are reluctant to have a parish council. Yet good leadership cannot be exercised nowadays without public discussion of ideas and shared planning for the future. Leadership today at all levels of business and politics is conducted by open discussion before the leader takes the necessary decisions. It is easy to poke fun at committees, but they are the only way human beings can be associated with the decision-making processes which affect their lives. A leader who deprives himself of advice and reaction from his flock is impoverishing himself and them disastrously. The bishops' pamphlet says: 'The faithful should be associated with the decision-making processes at diocesan and parish level, and means should be instituted to make this possible' (*Life in Communion*, para. 3). I think one of the reasons we priests fight shy of parish councils is the fear of possible conflict and public disagreement, which we think somehow is not Christian. It is a very natural fear, but not one any leader can afford to indulge. It is certainly not unchristian. In fact, conflict is often the best way to inaugurate true Christian understanding and peace between human beings. If we run away from short-term conflict in our parishes, the disagreements will not disappear; they will go underground where we have shovelled them and fester. We will have deprived ourselves of willing partners and created unhappy factions and opponents.

Some priests are reluctant to welcome religious sisters as equal partners in their parish work. In one deanery of the diocese parish sisters were welcomed as equal partners at deanery meetings for two years, but then, with a change of personnel among the priests, they were sent away and have not returned. The priests did not want to discuss deanery matters with the sisters. They did not think of the sisters as equal partners. At the Craiglockhart Day for Religious on Canon Law there was a round of applause from all the sisters present for the suggestion that they should attend deanery meetings. I think priests would be wise to recognize this genuine desire among our pastoral colleagues for partnership. We should surely invite them to meals with ourselves, plan pastoral work together, call each other by our Christian names, in fact, be friendly! From there it would be but a step towards doing the same with our parish councillors, and the 'demise of the clergyman' would be well under way. The concept of the clergyman, which is not in the gospels, was no doubt useful in its day and valuable for most of the first two thousand years of Christianity, but I am sure that in the next two thousand years it will be harmful to the spread of the gospel, and will be discarded – in fact, it is being discarded in many parts of the Church already. Thank God, for it is an obstacle to shared responsibility.

Some priests are reluctant to share their liturgical ministry with their parishioners. We tend to do it all ourselves, and so, once again, deprive ourselves of the enrichment of other people's ideas and partnership. The pamphlet *Life in Communion* sees as encouraging signs 'the active participation of the laity in the preparation and presentation of the liturgy and prayer life of the parish; the introduction of lay ministries' (para. 7). It should surely be standard practice in our parishes to have a liturgy committee which plans the public prayer life of the parish and shares with the celebrant the reactions of the parish to his celebration. As for the introduction of lay ministries I know of one parish where the formation of a band of lay eucharistic ministers has produced four vocations to the priesthood in four years which cannot be a bad thing. One reason for this was that they chose teenagers and young people as well as the middle-aged to become ministers of Holy Communion.

This brings me to a further point. Priests must be careful to incorporate into the groups of assistants who help serve the parish not just middle-aged and middle-class people. Inevitably in the world of talk, discussion, planning, such people will have a valuable part to play, but if we confine our sharing about the parish merely to them we run the risk of creating a new type of lay clergy, respectable, middle-class and unrepresentative. This can only be avoided by bringing the poor, the unemployed, the teenagers, the 'ordinary' into our councils and preventing the middle class from dominating them. Easier said than done. But, in my opinion, very important. I say this in all charity: look at the average Church of Scotland Kirk Session and see the perils before they come upon us.

One last point. Let us take plenty of risks and make plenty of mistakes. Only that way will we learn together with our laity what Christ wants of us for the future. Also, surely it is only by taking risks that we can become the saints Our Lord wants us to be. As Charles de Foucauld said, 'The absence of risk is a sure sign of mediocrity.'

10

Team Ministry in City Parishes

City parish

Catholic liturgy has undergone many changes in the last
fifteen years, but the biggest change has been the reintro-
duction of a sense of community in our celebrations. Before
1965 going to mass, although externally a communal act,
was internally an individualistic act: you were going to
communion, in which you met Our Lord personally, and
spoke to him in your heart. At communion other people
were a distraction. Going to mass now is not like that.
From the moment you enter the door of the Church till
the time you leave you are encouraged to notice your fellow
worshippers, to get involved with them, to feel part of
a community at worship. Both externally and internally
Catholics at mass are now encouraged to regard each other
not as distractions to proper worship, but as fellow worshippers to be sung with, prayed with, even laughed with.
When I was young I used to visit an aunt who was a nun
in a teaching order. I attended the nuns' mass in the
mornings (from a side chapel) and retain a memory of
seeing the sisters processing up to the altar rails for Holy
Communion, receiving the host, then proceeding back to
their places very slowly, eyes cast down, their heads now
enwrapped in thick black veils, totally cut off from everyone
else. As an adolescent I used to wonder how they saw their

way back to their places, since their heads were enshrouded front and back. But I knew that that was the proper way to go to communion – with eyes only for Our Lord. If I now attend mass with that same congregation of sisters the transformation is striking. The sisters gather round the altar, have eye contact with each other and the celebrant all through the canon of the mass, and at communion sing a communal song, perhaps even holding hands together. For them, now, celebrating mass is an act in common. They evidently consider each other not as distractions to the proper reception of Holy Communion, but as aids. They live a community life, so they want their mass to be a community celebration and they do all in their power to make it so.

Parish life today is dedicated to the same ideal. Priests know that Sunday mass is still the centre of Catholic life, that the Sunday coming together of the parish is the religious highlight of the week. Like the nuns they follow Vatican II in trying to make the parish mass a genuinely communal celebration. By and large, with lots of false experiments and failures, I think we succeed. At least we have set our feet in the right direction and are trying to emphasize the sense of community in parish liturgy, though most, if not all, of us have a long way to go.

The more difficult question for priests is the one following on from community liturgy. Can we in any way speak of a community life in our parishes in between Sunday liturgies? Even if Sunday mass is a joyfully communal affair, will those parishioners retain any sense of community from Monday to Saturday in their ordinary working lives? I have no doubt that the pre-motor car country parish of the past *was* a genuine community, every day of the week, not just on Sunday, so that Sunday mass could be an effortless expression of the common life of the parishioners. But I write from and for Catholics in a big city parish, such as is found all over western Europe, with no natural community to back it up. In a modern city parish, how possible is it to have a 'parish life' in between Sundays?

Personally I think parish community life is still possible in our big cities as long as we put aside nostalgia for the past and recognize that city life is quite different from country life. In city life any individual belongs to several communities, not just one. He or she probably belongs to a family which is their primary community. If they work they each belong to another community (factory, office, school). The neighbourhood they live in is another community (street, square, crescent). Their friends form a fourth community, often quite distinct from their neighbours. In the UK, class as well as preference is an important element here. A fifth and sixth separate community can be formed by hobbies (e.g. dancing or bowling) and age-group (especially for teenagers and old-age pensioners). City man and woman belong, in fact, to many communities and move between them with ease and flexibility. It is all very different from life in Donegal or in Ars at the time of St John Vianney. Therefore parish life has to be different.

In city life today parishes have to acknowledge that they are only one of several communities to which their parishioners belong. Another way to put this is to say that the people who come to church on Sunday, whom we encourage to form community among themselves, will accept that community life as one more, but not the only, community they belong to. They will continue to make their friends, to mix at work, to seek their recreation outside the strictly Catholic community of the parish. If the parish tries to absorb all their life, they will resist – usually by the simple feet-voting way of drifting away. If the parish does not get exalted ideas of itself but knows itself to be one among many communities its members belong to, there is scope for much important community-building, especially in the field of adult catechesis. Perhaps the best way to sum up what I have been trying to express is to say that parochial clergy must ask from their parishioners 100 per cent commitment to Jesus Christ as his disciples, but for none of those parishioners will that discipleship be 100 per cent commitment to the parish. Each will serve Christ in a variety of communities, only one of which is the local parish. The city parish community, then, is a wonderful variety of Christian commitments between Monday and Saturday which comes together on Sunday to express this variety at the grace-given point of unity – the Sunday Eucharist.

Is there any possibility, then, for a parish community as such? Lest I have given the impression that it is not possible, I hasten to say that it is. Among all those parishioners, busily involved in other communities, it is still desirable to gather them into strictly Catholic parochial groups, precisely in order to help them be better disciples of Christ in their non-parochial groupings. The modern city parish has a special emphasis on equipping its members for all the occasions when they are not gathered in a parish context. There is a strong formative element to be found. This is best done in groups. So parish life today tends to have many small groupings, besides the large Sunday grouping of the liturgy. Groups for prayer, liturgy preparation, Bible study, Christian discussion and formation, ecumenical contact and work, justice and peace promotion, Third World conscientization, social welfare all play their part in parish life. Parish social life tends to be experienced not in itself (parish socials) but as a spin-off from gathering together for apostolic and formative purposes. Consequently parish life is lived more in people's homes away from the centre than in the old type of parish hall next door to the church. In the same way weekday mass is frequently celebrated in houses away from the central church. All this adds up to a quiver-full activity in the parish, with a strong centrifugal tendency away from the parish centre out into the homes and lives of the parishioners. This prompts questions: Who services and co-ordinates this activity? Who keeps it all together?

An intermediate answer to the question is a strong parish council. This should be the body which invites all the active groups in the parish to send representatives so as to form a meeting which both co-ordinates present and inspires future activity. It is, ideally, an assembly which acts as a clearing house for information (see), a meeting to discern what is best for the parish (judge) and a body which sees that all does not end at words and that action is taken (act). It is made up of parishioners, the parishioners who devote much of their time and energies between Sundays to forming and working for the parish community. All parishes have these generously inclined persons whose dedication to Jesus Christ does lead them to give a large amount of time to the parish. I will not here expand on the subject of parish councils which is a subject on its own. I mention them as a necessary element in parish community life, especially in city parishes with their huge potential for Christian activity. Without a parish council it would be very difficult for the priests to co-ordinate parish activities and keep them healthily engaged. Not just difficult, surely impossible.

Team ministry

I am convinced that the modern city parish, as sketched above, needs a team ministry, and that a priest on his own cannot do justice to it. Parishioners, as I have said, must not be expected to equate their commitment to Christ with their commitment to the parish, because of the non-parochial spheres they belong to which are part of their Christian life. But that is not to say there cannot be a group at the centre of the parish who do equate their Christian commitment with commitment to the parish. These are the full-time ministers of the parish. While they are in the parish their Christian task is to work full-time in it. They are at the service of the parish community. They are called to serve and make all other interests secondary to that service; all their life centres on the parish.

In the past, such ministers have always been ordained priests. But that need not be so. The team at the centre of the parish, its ministers, need not all be ordained (male) priests. In fact in a city the team functions best when there is the widest possible variety in its make-up; variety of sex (men and women), variety of age (from 20 to 60 plus), variety of talents, interests and bees-in-the-bonnet, variety of background and role (ordained, not ordained). The wider the variety in the team the greater the possibility for ministry. Each single team-member has an attraction for some but not for others, has special gifts equipping him or her for special work, has special interests which make him or her want to do things which others do not want to do, has a unique background which enables him or her to go where others cannot. And so on. The richer the variety, the greater the potential for ministry. So, today, in parish teams you find sisters working alongside priests, trained in ministries which priests are not trained in, like social work or catechetics, and—above all providing the feminine element in the parish ministry which has been missing in the past.

In our parish for the last few years we have also had young lay persons in our team. These young men have come to us for a year or two to give voluntary service in the team, usually after university education and before going on to work and marriage. They have lived in the parish house with the rest of the team and have provided a lay dimension to our ministry which has proved invaluable. Without exception they have been accepted by parishioners. Theirs is an interesting vocation, about which we may hear more in the Church: to be full-time, celibate ministers but only for a period in their lives.

In a parish team there is a natural unity given by the unity of purpose of the team. All are engaged in ministry of this one parish. There is also, however, a natural disunity, given by that rich variety of types, talents, training, which I have mentioned. The richer the variety in the team the greater the potential for disunity in that team. It is good, for instance, to have a variety of ages in a parish team, but sixty-year-olds and twenty-five-year-olds do not always find working together easy. It is good for male priests trained in seminaries and female nuns formed in religious life to work together, but they do not always find each other understandable. It is good when members of the same team pursue separate interests like Charismatic Renewal and the Movement for a Better World, but that diversity makes for uneasy partnership in the apostolate. Each is tempted to think the other needs converting to his or her way. In other words, the drives for disunity in a parish team can be very strong. The positive element of variety in a team which enables its ministry to be far-reaching and attractive to many can overnight turn into a negative element of anger, frustration, even despair within the team. We have all, I suppose, come across such situations. An overworked parish priest has invited a group of sisters to help him in his parish. The sisters have responded enthusiastically. Pastoral work among families in the parish, living among the people in a non-institutional small house, life in the secular city away from the big religious institution – all these opportunities are just what they wanted. Mother Provincial is especially delighted that she can offer congenial work to her young sisters who have recently joined the congregation. But the team ministry thus lightly embraced has often proved unexpectedly difficult, as the hidden tensions provided by the differences in temperament, training, background, interest, theological and pastoral presumptions, and spiritual maturity have risen to the surface. It has often taken less than a year for an enthusiastically formed team to break up in sad despair.

At this point two observations need to be made. The first is that some people are simply not suitable for team work. They work, and live, better on their own. This has nothing to do with whether they are good or bad priests or Religious. It is a fact, like being left-handed or colour-blind. Such temperaments should be recognized and not asked to work in a team. This recognition, of course, sometimes comes after a year or two of team work. My second observation is that the difficulties in team work which so suddenly surface should never be occasions for despair. They do not spell the end of the experiment. In fact there is nothing wrong in their appearance. They are growth points in the coming together of the team, signs of maturity ahead, rather than signs of imminent break-up. However, for these tensions to be fruitful we have to react constructively and not miss the opportunities they hold for the group. I suggest that such constructive reaction involves three things: communication, prayer and respect.

Working in a team requires communication. Team members must share information about what they are doing, ideas about what needs to be done, healthy criticism about what is being done, and so on. Clearly a system of communication is needed, by which I mean formal meetings from time to time, properly conducted on business lines. This is especially so if the parish team does not live under one roof. Underlying the system of communication there needs to be, in all members, an ability and *desire* to share. This is not easy for some. Most of us have to make an effort to share our plans. We all have a liking for hugging secrets and not exposing ourselves too much to cold blasts from others. It is no secret that pre-Vatican-II training in seminaries and convents did not help us to communicate readily with our fellows. Add to this a few personal hang-ups – e.g. over women, or lay people, or young priests or old priests – and the difficulties in communication mount up. They have to be faced and overcome. If we are to be good servants at the heart of the parish we have to work hard to be a good team. Community in the parish team has a way of spreading into the parish contagiously. Unfortunately bad team work in the ministry cannot be hidden, and it too has repercussions in the parish. The desire and ability to communicate, then, is of paramount importance in a parish team. Without it the best system of communication by meetings, minutes, resolutions, feedback, etc., is practically useless. Sharing in the team starts in the hearts of the members. If I do not want to share, no amount of attendance at meetings will make me.

The deepest level of sharing is praying together. Secular priests have not in the past been expected to pray together, but Religious have. The latter are often surprised at the former's reluctance. I think team ministry requires us to do some praying together. To live together, work together, communicate together but not pray together is somehow insufficient. In our team we have tried various experiments, e.g. praying together at lunch every day, a prayer meeting on Saturday nights, or on a weekday afternoon. Currently we meet each night for Compline in someone's room and mull over the day together before and after the formal prayer. I find this a very soothing end to the day, especially if we have been busy and have not met much during it. I have heard of parish teams who from time to time celebrate a mass together with just themselves in the parish house. That sounds good.

Deeper even than the desire to communicate and the desire to share prayer with members of the parish team is a quality which is difficult to find one word for. It is the quality which makes a good marriage work. One word for it is respect. Working in a team one learns to respect the other members. You have to respect their talents, which are by definition different from your own, remembering that also by definition they are probably lacking in the talents which you possess (which you rate, of course, as very high). You have also to learn to give others plenty of space to work in, not barging into that space with unasked-for questions or, still worse, blundering criticisms. Currently I work with team members who proceed in quite different ways from my own and have, to my mind, mysterious priorities. I must resist the temptation to have it out with them and probe into their privacies which I sometimes long to do. Giving people space in which to be themselves is important. Another aspect of this respect for others is trust. Team members just have to trust each other, At work they must trust each other and not indulge in negative thoughts. At meetings they must trust each other,

117

especially when one is being critical of another. They must never be jealous, or arrogant, or rude. The list begins to look like St Paul's description in 1 Corinthians 13. In other words at the heart of the parish team, undergirding the meetings for communication and the sharing of work and prayer, there has to be Christian love. This love should be active in the parish team, and from there go out in waves to the entire parish community. It travels in the other direction too, thus forming a circle of love, a band of spiritual energy travelling through the parish back into and through the parish team and out again.

A word about the leader of the team. There are all types of leadership, depending on the make-up of the leader and the type of group he leads. A parish team is a small, intimate group. It requires an intimate, sharing sort of leadership more like the father of a family than the commander of an army. It seems to me that it is exercised more by just living and working together than by saying things. Directives are not really the best way to lead a small team, which eats at the same table and shares the chores. Natural and easy discussion as we eat together, showing a genuine interest in what we have each been doing all morning, honest airing of doubts about oneself and the parish, a bit of benevolent (not malevolent) teasing, plenty of laughter, especially against oneself – these are the sort of things which make up small-team leadership. Especially one must guard against becoming self-important or pretentious.

The last quality I suggest is the ability to take the strain of others. One has to enter into the moods and quirks of other people, and not indulge in too many moods oneself. One has never to run away from the suffering of others, always be available within the team, over and above the call of the parish outside. One has to *love* the brethren.

The biblical image of the Suffering Servant is helpful. He suffered that others might be liberated. By his wounds others were healed. He was a constructive lover, and it was to that image of a redeemer, who liberated others by lovingly suffering for them, that Jesus turned when he was searching for a model for his activity. Leaders in the Church today need look no further for their own model.

11

Depth of Silence

They say that after the revolution in 1917 the first thing the Russians wanted to do with their new freedom was to talk. People gathered at street corners, in homes, everywhere, not to do anything in particular, but just to talk. A similar thing happened to us in the Catholic Church after Vatican II. The log-jam in Catholic thinking was broken, and we began to talk. Think of the number of discussions, seminars, conferences which took place in the post-conciliar years as we adjusted to the challenge of *aggiornamento* and tried to work out the Church's future. Now, in the 1980s, we have settled down to a new maturity, and there is less talk and more prayer and action.

Nowhere was this talking phenomenon more evident than in the way priests reacted to their new freedom in the liturgy once the rubric-dominated mass of Pius V was gone. The change into English in the mass, combined with liberation from rubrics, produced an excessively talkative liturgy. Celebrants, young and old, brightly innovative young and garrulous old, began to punctuate their mass with sermonettes: 'As we begin mass let us. . .', 'Now we come to the offertory. The offertory is. . .', 'In exchanging the handshake of peace we. . .'. Even the precious silence after communion was interrupted with the celebrant's thoughts on how the people ought to be making their thanksgiving. Together with the sermonette came the commentary. Talkative celebrants began not only to preach their way through the mass but also to comment on what was happening. The priest saying mass became a compère as well as a celebrant. 'Now we sit to listen to the Word of God', 'Now we stand for the Gospel', 'Now we have the offertory procession'. A particular danger point was the Pax. Few of us got past that without an explanation about its meaning, oblivious that there are few things more self-explanatory than a handshake between human beings. But no, we had to talk and explain – and spoil.

The tragedy of this was that it was well-intentioned. It was not that priests talked for the sake of talking. I think we talked out of an excessive desire to make the mass 'interesting', a meaningful experience for those who came, instead of a dull fulfilment of duty. The intentions were good. I think it was the execution which was poor, or perhaps our values. We thought that to make the mass interesting we had to use words. It was the teacher instinct in many of us. We were, simultaneously, becoming conscious in our pastoral work of the need for adult education. This desire to educate spilled over into our celebration of the liturgy. Imperceptibly the mass became a teaching situation, the greatest educational opportunity of the week for the conscientious pastor of the flock. Educating our flocks by means of the liturgy became our overriding, not to say relentless, concern at the Sunday liturgy. There began to be a concentration on the liturgy of the Word, the teaching part of the mass, to the detriment of the liturgy of the Eucharist, where we participate in Christ's act. I have been to Sunday masses where the liturgy of the Word took 40 minutes and the canon of the mass was over in 10 minutes. We dwelt for long in the ante-chamber and scurried through the Presence. Another thing that happened was the appearance of 'teaching-aids' on the walls of the church and the sanctuary: pictures and captions, frequently done by children, in explanation of the day's gospel or the season of the year. The church began to take on the appearance of an up-to-date classroom, which was not surprising, since liturgical committees at parish and diocesan level tend to have a disproportionate number of teachers on them.

A third parallel thing occurred. The non-verbal communication of symbols and actions, which is the glory of Catholic liturgy, began to take second place to verbal communication. I have already mentioned how the Pax was seldom negotiated without an explanatory sermonette. But if you *explain* a symbol, you have robbed it of its power by slowing down its momentum. If I love you, I kiss you. It would be absurdly didactic and non-productive to explain why I was kissing you before I did so. The act is its own explanation. So it is with religious acts. Catholic liturgy is replete with such symbols and actions which operate at a semi-conscious level, deeper than words, not fully explainable in words. To start trying to explain them is somehow to flatten them, and to turn what is a mystery (which has no solution) into a problem (which has a solution). There was an example of this desire to put things into words in our parish last year. The sanctuary of the church has a striking life-size crucifix by Arthur Pollen hanging above the altar and dominating the church. One month last year our liturgical committee erected behind the sanctuary a huge notice in primary colours 'GOD IS LOVE'. This notice not only distracted from the action of the mass but also could not hope to be as effective as the crucifix in conveying the central message. Sometimes to substitute words for symbols is to evaporate the mystery. A line from Edwin Muir about the calvinist services of his youth springs to mind. 'The Word made flesh here has been made word again.'

We need to regain the truth that liturgical celebration is primarily worship of God, participation in the eternal mystery of Christ; and only secondarily is it meant to be listening to the Word of God and teaching the flock. The liturgy of the Word has its place in every sacrament, but that place is secondary to and supportive of the main action. If we grasp that, there will be less danger that we drown the paschal work of Christ in a torrent of words. We will begin to let the actions of the liturgy, especially of the mass, speak for themselves – they are magnificently eloquent if performed with respect. This means relearning the value of silence in liturgy. For leaders of liturgy and celebrants it means being secure enough not to fuss with words or try to improve upon traditionally consecrated formulas and actions. Keep quiet, adore, contemplate, and let the Word and Sacrament take over is a good prescription for liturgical leaders. We are there, in the presence of One greater than us, to be catalysts of his presence and action, conductors of his grace for the people. We are not to be busy actors in the centre of the stage, obscuring by talk the work of the sacrament. Rather we have to take a back seat and let Christ act through us. He must increase, while we decrease.

Anyone who has sat on a committee knows that the way to gain attention is not by talking a lot but by remaining silent till the chatter is over and we are asked for a contribution. In the same way the best way to control a noisy room is not to shout louder than anyone else, which only increases the turmoil, but to restore law and order by quietness and silence. I have learned from observing colleagues who have success with young people. I notice that they do not raise their voices or act like sergeant-majors. They seem to say little, but they listen much, and lead by participating non-verbally. In similar ways celebrants lead the liturgy most effectively when they are deeply conscious of the presence of Christ, and are not afraid to say nothing. I say 'not afraid', because I think it needs some poise and courage to curb one's tongue and allow silence to prevail. A voice inside one urges one to fill the void with a word of explanation or an improving thought. It is nearly always better to say nothing on these insecure occasions. After all, Christ is present. He can be relied upon to fill silence and transform it from barren awkwardness to rich meaning. Silence is an opportunity for the direct action of the Spirit upon the members of the congregation, each of whom is a distinct person with distinct needs coming from a distinct background and going to a goal which is unique to himself. In such a setting words are only partially successful in uniting, whereas silence can be deeply unitive just because it does not intrude.

In our ecclesial life we have on the whole settled down into more mature, less talkative, action than fifteen years ago when the excitement of *aggiornamento* first hit us. It is my prayer that this new maturity will grow in the liturgy. To do this we priests have to be more confident about the mass than we have been in the recent past. When people say they find the mass boring, it is right that we should examine our consciences about our parish liturgy, but we must be careful not to react in panic with a show-biz flurry of words and music. It is possible that that sort of remark is really telling us about the spiritual state of the critic rather than the state of our liturgy. We should be trying to lead people to a deeper understanding of what the paschal mystery is. Sometimes it is bad pastoral strategy to make the liturgy noisy in order to attract more people, because the noisiness leads people away from considerations of themselves and God, so that though they may be in church their attendance there is not helping them to grow.

Fifty years ago Romano Guardini wrote his seminal *The Spirit of the Liturgy*. In my opinion, what he wrote is still valid today. On the subject of restraint he wrote:

> The restraint characteristic of the liturgy is at times very pronounced – so much so as to make this form of prayer appear at first as a frigid intellectual production, until we gradually grow familiar with it and realise what vitality pulsates in the clear, measured forms. And how necessary this discipline is! At certain moments and on certain occasions it is permissible for emotions to have a vent. But a prayer which is intended for the everyday use of a large body of people must be restrained.

My point in quoting the words is not to make a plea for dull liturgy which simultaneously harms nobody and inspires nobody. My point has been to try to show that ultimately the dullest liturgy is that very liturgy which is trying to be interesting by piling on the words and 'happenings', whereas the most exciting liturgy is the liturgy where restraint is exercised and the depths of the mystery of Christ are allowed to predominate, through restraint on the part of the human actors. As a pagan Red Indian once said, 'Silence is the great mystery. The holy silence is God's voice. If you ask what are the fruits of silence, God will say: they are self-control, true courage or endurance, patience, dignity and reverence. Silence is the cornerstone of character.' We need such character in our celebration of the liturgy.

12

Spiritual Formation Today

SHARING NOT GIVING

One of the stories I was brought up with was the story of St Martin. He was a Roman soldier and a Christian. One cold winter's night he was riding along in uniform on his horse when he saw at the side of the road a beggar who had no clothes and was freezing cold. St Martin stopped and, having pity for the man, he took off his own cloak and, with his sword, cut the cloak in two. He gave half to the beggar and kept half for himself. He then went on his way. The story goes on: that night St Martin had a dream in which Jesus Christ came to him wearing the half-cloak he had given to the beggar. That is a very telling story. But I remember thinking, when I was young: Why did St Martin not give the whole of his cloak? Would it not have been more noble, a better example to us all, more sensitive, to give the whole cloak? However, more recently I have perceived that giving half the cloak contains the essence of Christianity, because this was *sharing*. St Martin was coming down to the same level as the beggar. He was saying: I'm cold too. You and I can share this cloak. I am not going just to give you the cloak, I am going *to share* it with you. Deep at the centre of Christianity and of the life you and I lead is the notion not so much of giving but of *sharing with each other*.

When you give you are a benefactor; when you share you are a participant and equal. For instance, I have here a morning roll. If I were a benefactor I would give you the roll. Having done that you would walk away and I would walk away. We are not involved with one another. But if I share the roll, giving you half and keeping half myself . . . what have we done? We have shared the bread, we have broken the bread together, we have become involved with one another, we have set up an Emmaus community and we eat the roll together. I think it is important to see that sharing involves being involved.

Benefactors give their name. All over Scotland one can see names like Carnegie. But Carnegie didn't get involved with the libraries that his money built. He had the money to spare, and that was that. But you and I must exercise our Christianity by sharing with people our time, talents, love and feelings. Jesus, at the Last Supper, said: 'The kings of the Gentiles exercise lordship over them; and those in authority over them are called benefactors. But not so with you' (Luke 22:25). A moment later Jesus took the bread, broke it and gave it to his followers and friends. At the heart of your religion and mine is the sign of the broken and shared bread.

A human aspect of the whole divine plan of salvation – the incarnation – is Jesus, the Son of God, sharing our human life. The whole of Pentecost is the Spirit of God coming down and being shared among us. There is no giving. God did not redeem man from on high like a thunderbolt; he came himself and shared thirty-three years of life, of toil and tears, of labour, joy and happiness, of expectations, dreads and despairs. He shared. 'By the mystery of this water and wine may we come to share in the divinity of Christ, who humbled himself to share in our humanity.' That is a significant and important prayer to sum up the following of Christ.

Perhaps you and I can go a little deeper now into the meaning of the broken bread. It seems to me that when you share three things happen: you have broken; you have created a community by eating what you have broken; and you experience joy. That comes from eating together and the community thereby created. You and I can look into our lives and think of times when we have shared: a confidence, time, a trouble, a happiness with somebody. Something inside you had to give way – an inherited inhibition or something rather difficult to talk about. Perhaps it was difficult to give time – you had to break your day's programme when someone came into your life unexpectedly. But by breaking that programme you created a community and experienced joy.

Those who are in the teaching profession know that the essence of good teaching is to share – it is not just for me to give you information. It is walking together along the path of knowledge, with one person better informed, but all of us getting to know each other as we go along. I can remember a phrase from Frank Sheed over forty years ago when, as a resident speaker at Hyde Park Corner, he would say: 'What must I do to teach John Latin? First of all I must know John, secondly I must know Latin.' It is creating a community, it is a sharing of your personality with people that makes for good teaching and good Christianity.

All those who belong to religious communities, either Religious in the strict sense or parish communities, know that at the heart of an active and happy parish is sharing: when the priest is able to share information like details of finance with his people; able to share plans, so that it is not just him making the plans and others implementing them, but getting together round a table and sharing the planning, moving forward together. A priest of my generation has had to learn that! Thirty years ago there was scarcely a notion of Catholic parishes sharing information about money, pastoral plans, etc., and not much mutual trust between priest and people. But now we have learned, often the hard way of being broken at times, that a good, lively parish is one where you risk being hurt, being depressed, being happy – for happiness is a risk too. You risk these things in order to move forward in the parish. This is the way Christ bears fruit in our lives and in our parish communities.

Mention of fruit makes me think of Our Lord's great parable in John's Gospel, of the vine and the branches. This rings lots of bells with me because it is a marvellous invitation to share. Christ is saying: 'Now that my phase of active redemption is over, in which I lived and taught, cared for people, and died, I have risen and am ascended to heaven to the Father. Now that I send my Spirit to the nascent Church *you* will do these things, because I am the vine and you are the branches!' When you look at a vine you see that the luscious bunches of grapes grow at the end of the branches, not on the parent stem. That says wonderful things to me: that says Christ is going to bear fruit through me. What he did he still does, through you, through me. The bearing of the fruit is the sharing of the sap that makes the bunches of grapes grow, through the parent stem, through the branches, acting together. All the things we do, Christ did. When Christ was on earth he cared for people, he healed people, he talked to people, he listened to people, he inspired people, he liberated them and set them free. Now he says: 'Go and do likewise.' We are invited to be Christ in our generation. All the activities

129

that Christ will do in this world will be done through us, the branches of the vine, and not by some kind of magic.

You and I must have had many experiences when we felt Christ working through us. A few years ago a parishioner came to me and said his wife Peggy had been suddenly taken to hospital with cancer, and would I go and see her. Peggy was not a Catholic, she was not even a Christian. When I went to see her in hospital she was in considerable pain, and at the end of the visit I asked her: 'May I give you my blessing?' She said: 'Certainly.' That afternoon John came to the house and said: 'I don't know what you did for Peggy but she wants to see you again. She has been quite different since you visited her.' He said that when I blessed her (which I regret had been a perfunctory, courteous gesture of a priest) she felt something happen. She was asking to become a Christian and a Catholic. So I baptized her, received her into the Church, and anointed her. She died the next day. I give you this example because it shows Christ working through me, almost without my co-operation. I had just done the polite thing.

But there are times when we stop Christ working through us, and that is a change from the vine and the branches. Christ is not going to bypass his Church (by that I mean his faithful people). He is going to work through those branches and if I, through laziness, pride or false humility, fail to do something I should do, for Christ, then I silence him. If I should be listening, but do not, I stop Christ listening; if I should be speaking up, but do not, through fear, I have silenced Christ.

Being the vine and the branches: you either act or you do not. You can allow the Spirit to move in you, or you can silence the Spirit. Miracles apart, this is how Christ is saving the world; no other way. It is a crazy way of doing it, but it is what he chose: sharing. Sharing is the essence of the apostolate of Christ.

Christ suffered. But he no longer suffers, at the right hand of the Father, in his own person; he suffers through you and me. Pascal said: 'Christ is in agony until the end of time.' Not his agony, in his glorified body, but your agony and my agony, in our sufferings. This is a marvellous thing: none of us is excluded from working for the kingdom. We may not be active, indeed we may be very inactive, through no fault of our own – through circumstances, through the effect of passing years; but we can still, in the spirit of St Thérèse of Lisieux, offer everything to the Kingdom. This is a very inspiring message: that you and I can both act for Christ and act with Christ; that we can suffer for Christ, and suffer with Christ, in the promotion of the kingdom of God in this world. Lastly, as well as acting through suffering, we can *pray*. Christ, in this life, prayed so much: nights spent in prayer, forty days in the desert, times with his apostles when he took them aside to pray. A busy man by day, a prayerful man by night, he is inviting you and me to do the same. Of the three this is the key: if you and I are not giving ourselves in prayer, if deep in our heart the Spirit of God is not moving, then our passion and our actions, our suffering and our working for the kingdom will be dreadfully superficial. We must pray. Here we touch the very heart of the apostolate of Christ. There we pray easily, we adore, we intercede, we do penance, we say: 'Abba'. All for salvation and the promotion of the kingdom of God in this world. Prayer touches our heart; prayer melts our heart. Deep within my heart the Spirit dwells and prays with me and for me.

One of my favourite prophecies in the Old Testament, of the coming of the Kingdom (when the Messiah would come), is Ezekiel's marvellous description of God's promise: I will pour my Spirit upon mankind and I will put away your hearts of stone and give you hearts of flesh.' I have sometimes thought that, if I had been the prophet Ezekiel, I would have had it the other way round! I would have said: 'When the kingdom comes I shall tear away your weak and unreliable hearts of flesh and give you hearts of stone – sturdy like a rock'. 'Thou art Peter, and on this rock I will build my Church.' Rock is something solid and dependable. But Ezekiel did not say that! No, take away that hardness and self-confidence, that security in yourself, and I will give you a heart of flesh, that can be hurt, that is vulnerable, that can weep, that can be unsure of itself, because you are going to be able to love; and love is full of all these things. As well as being excitedly ecstatic, love can also weep, be shy and diffident.

Christian action, then, is done by you and me, ordinary people with weak and wobbly hearts who do not have the security of trained skills, etc. I think Christian action and the promotion of the kingdom is done by those who are afraid of what people will say, who are a bit cowardly, who are a bit diffident about standing up in public, do not have the security of plenty of practice and experience, can be capsized by failure, hurt by remarks, hurt by being ignored; find themselves reacting jealously when they do not want to, are overcome with despair, yet go on loving and trusting. It is the weak and wobbly hearts that Christ chooses, as he chose Peter, James, John, Thomas – all the disciples. They were not the high-fliers of Galilee or Judaea, they were the ordinary folk, capable of love.

This new heart that God gives us, through the gift of the Spirit, is not going to transform us into super people; we shall be the same, but with big horizons, big capabilities, because we have the Spirit of God dwelling deep in our hearts. Christ says: 'You ordinary folk must now have the highest standards. I am not reducing the standards because you are a poor lot. I am keeping the standards high and asking you to aim ceaselessly for them.' 'You must love one another,' Christ said at the Last Supper, 'as I have loved you.' I often reflect and meditate on that phrase: '. . . as Christ loved us . . .'. It seems to me there are two special marks of Jesus Christ's loving.

First, Christian loving is always the first to love. It doesn't say: when you earn my respect, prove yourself to be important, I'll love you. No, Christian love says: I'll love you now, even if you are not very attractive, even if you don't particularly like me, even if you don't have a notable future. In other words, Christian love is creative; it is the first to love. John in his epistle says: 'God first loved us.' God says to you and me: be the first to go out and love all men and women.

There is a nice phrase from St John of the Cross: 'Where there is no love, put love, and there love will lead.' That is a great motto for parishes! Often in parishes people come along and say: I can't work with him or her – they're snobs, they're a clique, they pay no attention to me. Or: I can't work with that priest, he's brusque, etc. There's no love in him, Father. The answer is: Do not say there is no love in him; say, where is the love in me? Where there is no love, put love. A Christian does not wait for the ideal situation. A lot of people wait for the ideal parish and then say: It's great to be in it. Ideal parishes are the fruit of labour and prayer; they are not the 'givenness' of any of us. They are not given to us; we labour through grace to create. Where there is no love put love, and there love will lead. You may not see it, but it will come. That is the first mark of Christian love.

The second mark of Christian love is that Christian love never stops. It is the first to love and the last to stop. It

never stops. Shakespeare put this very well. He said in one
of his sonnets: 'Love is not love which alters when it alteration finds.' This is very profound. It is very easy to start
off when things are going well; and then we all get on each
other's nerves, we have no success, the glamour goes a bit
and the parish priest is moved, or the person who helped
us is gone and we find it difficult to keep going. But that
is not love. Love keeps going.

Another name for love in the Old Testament is fidelity,
faithfulness. All married people can tell us that married
life is a school of fidelity and faithfulness. Love is not love
at all if it alters when it alteration finds.

So, these are the high standards. We must love one
another, said Christ, as I have loved you – being the first
to start and never to stop. That is an immense programme,
a huge ideal.

Christianity has high ideals, but low practice on the
whole. There is always an uncomfortable gap between our
ideals and our practice which makes us feel guilty and
awkward. We do not like to live with that gap between
practice and promise.

There are two ways of closing that gap and stopping
the pain. One way is to lower the ideals. Imperceptibly,
sometimes, down they come. Then, up comes the practice
a bit and we feel comfortable. We may not notice that our
ideals have been lowered, but they have. But, this is not
Christ's way of solving that problem. Christ's way is to
keep the ideals as high as heaven: 'Thy kingdom come, thy
will be done.' We only have to remember the Sermon on
the Mount: 'Turn the other cheek', 'Forgive a man seventy
times seven', 'Don't be anxious about the future' – all these
colossally impossible ideals of Matthew, chapters 5, 6, and
7 . . . But keep going! We fall, we rise; we have the forgive-
ness of God, the sacrament of reconciliation, Holy

Communion; we attend mass and pray daily. We rise and we fall. There is always a gap, but we have not committed the one treason of lowering the ideals. The message is clear: not to lower the ideals but to raise ceaselessly the practice to those high ideals. In the heart of Christ, we can do it! Without him, clearly we do not and we cannot.

Our Lord promised: 'Greater things you will do than I have done.' How does that bit of the gospel seem to you? All right for Peter and Paul, but not for you? Even with this gap, the vine can still produce these bunches of grapes. If we have humble hearts, if we pray, if we never give in, if, especially, we have *hope*.

LETTING GO TO GOD

We can go a little deeper into that metaphor of the vine and the branches, the symbol of our salvation. Firstly, it is communal. We may think of the saving of our own soul, but then we are missing the larger picture. It is not just me and God in Christ saving my soul. It is us, all together, saving the world. At Pentecost, we look to the Holy Spirit. We ask the Holy Spirit to help us 'renew the face of the earth'. Nothing about renewing you and me. That is taken for granted. My renewal takes place as I 'renew the face of the earth'. There is no limit to that! This is something I do myself, even in Christ; it is something we do, in Christ.

The phrase 'in Christ' is mentioned so many times in St Paul's epistles; let us think on this for a few moments. The New Testament does not speak of salvation 'by Christ', it speaks of salvation 'in Christ'. What is the difference? Let me give a crude example: I sometimes play golf. Sometimes I hit the ball at the fourth tee down the fairway. The ball has been hit by me. Suppose that when I hit the ball I went with the ball to where it landed . . . That would be continuous contact, all the way through the shot. This is a parallel of what salvation in Christ is. You and I were not just saved 'by Christ' 2,000 years ago and it's all over on Christ's part. We are being saved *now* 'in Christ'. There is a continuous transaction between the saving power of Christ, through his spirit and myself, in my soul. It is a continuous transaction. It is love. Love isn't like hitting the ball and walking away. Love is sharing. Love goes with you all the time. Christ's love for me, and my love for Christ – a continuous transaction. I'm being saved. More exciting: I'm being sanctified, all the time. If it is not over yet, that is fine. That means the presence of Christ is still needed by me. His presence in me, saving me, will go on, in this continuous transaction of love, when we share each other's ideals and life.

But that does not explain what the whole of salvation means. We have just said the first part: I am saved and sanctified continuously in Christ. But salvation, renewing the face of the earth, is all about saving and sanctifying in Christ. Not just being saved, but saving and sanctifying us all, to renew the face of the earth. It is these two things going on all the time: being saved and saving, being sanctified and sanctifying. Cardinal Suenens said recently. 'Christians are people who go out, do not just stay in.' They save and sanctify all the time or they do not, as the case may be, but their mission is to be saved and saving, to be sanctified and sanctifying, all the time.

The two technical terms for being saved and saving are grace and mission. These are indispensable unities. The breathing in and out of my heart, in Christ. You never get one without the other in the Bible. The prophet Isaiah, called in the Temple, saved. God touches him: Holy, Holy, Holy. Then God says, 'Whom shall I send?' Isaiah answers, 'Send me!' The grace of his conversion has made him say, 'Send me.'

I like the picture which St Luke gives of Jesus on Mount Tabor, taking his three special friends up the mountain to pray. When he prayed he was so overwhelmed by the presence of God that he was transfigured. It was such a marvellous moment that Peter said: 'Let's be here for ever. Let's build three temples. Let's stay here.' But, 'No!' says Christ, 'Down the mountain we go and set out on our way to Jerusalem.' Immediately, at the foot of the mountain Jesus is involved once more in saving and sanctifying, this time of an epileptic boy. Grace on the mountain top, mission at the foot of the mountain, on the road to Jerusalem. A holy ecstasy sent Jesus out to a very ordinary task of caring and healing, healing the epileptic boy and comforting his father.

What can you and I say about grace, except let us open ourselves to it? Let us pray. Let the Spirit of God overwhelm us. Let us be taken over by the Spirit of God. Let go, into God's hands. Someone asked if I could explain how this is done. I cannot, because it is not a technique, and woe betide anyone who thinks it is! It is just an act of generosity, day by day, week by week. You cannot learn the technique of letting go to God, you just let it happen. Let go! It is as simple and challenging as that. Let our conversion take place by letting go, in the Spirit of God. Let us be overwhelmed by the Spirit. It is not the Spirit that holds back. It is not that God's arm is foreshortened. It is our weakness and lack of generosity, our being distracted, that prevents the Lord from taking over completely every nook and cranny of our life.

I have spoken on other occasions about giving time. How much time do we give to God in prayer? What about half an hour a week? Most of us live on a weekly cycle rather than a daily cycle. If you live in the country you have a daily cycle: you milk the cows and do other farm tasks every day. But most of us live in cities, where you will notice our cycle of living is a weekly one. You fill up the larder and deep-freeze once a week. You take the children out on a Saturday, once a week. Could it not be that we are missing out on our time of prayer because we say, every day, I am too busy. Maybe I am too busy every day, but every week I am not too busy for the half-hour or hour that is asked of us. Start with once a week, on a Saturday; just as you shop, so often, on a Saturday, so you could take your New Testament, go to church, draw apart and pray for half an hour. I mention these nitty-gritty things, because there is always the danger of talking generalizations. Why not allow grace to take over for that half-hour a week, coupled with the Sunday liturgy and day-to-day prayer that you learned at your mother's knee?

Grace is followed by mission. To save is the sanctifying of the world; it is to produce the fruit at the end of the branches of the parent stem. I think this is done by being present. You cannot save the world *in absentia*, at a distance. The Son of God did not save the world at a distance, he shared our life and conditions. You and I do not save people without being in contact with them and present to them.

A statement by Albert Camus is relevant here: 'Don't walk in front of me, I may not follow. Don't walk behind me, I may not lead. Walk beside me and be my friend.' That's the only kind of leadership that modern people understand. Not the exalted leadership from above, not the dragging behind of pusillanimous people who are cowardly, but walking hand-in-hand, opening the Word of God, being lightened by Christ and mixing with people.

Inevitably this brings us back to prayer and I must

admit that while I have always tried to base my life on prayer, I have noticed a remarkable change in my attitude to it recently. I have always desired mystical union with God, because that is what I feel my baptism calls me to. For many years I thought mystical union with God meant being slightly detached, slightly impassive, sharing in God's tranquillity and peace, above the struggle of this world, and I hoped that would happen. But I have learnt from the New Testament and from experience that mystical union with God gives you, in St Paul's marvellous phrase, the mind of Christ. By prayer working on our baptism you and I are given the mind of Christ. And the mind of Christ is not remote, impassive, above the struggle; the mind of Christ, the heart of Christ, is full of compassion for people suffering, sorrow for people's sins, anger at man's inhumanity to man, and injustice, sensitivity to the needs of the downtrodden and marginalized, desiring above all reconciliation between men, a certain seriousness about the condition of this world. The mind of Christ takes sides: for justice, against injustice; for peace, against war. There is no compromise in the mind of Christ.

I have discovered that praying gives you the mind of Christ. It does not give you peace and tranquillity about the struggle. It gives you a deep seriousness about God's world. Into his beautiful world God put man, to develop it and fructify. But see what a mess we are making of it! Christ does not just walk away at this. He is angry at times; he is desperately upset; he is sensitive. Read the prophets, read the psalms, read Jesus himself, read St Paul . . . There is nothing tranquil and Buddha-like about the Christian God. We have learnt that from the Jewish God. Prayer gives you God's view, not the whole of it or we would be burnt up, but enough to be disturbed. People said about Jesus that he came to comfort the disturbed,

139

but disturb the comfortable. This is exactly what praying does to me, and I'm sure it does this to you also. He comforts me; but he also disturbs me.

He disturbs me when I see the imbalance in our world, the imbalance between north and south, the struggle between east and west, the pettiness of man, the structural injustice of our planet. You and I walk into our supermarkets and buy tea, coffee, sugar, fruit, fruit juice . . . They are there on our shelves as a buyable presence; but they are the end of a big chain of multinational commerce. At the other end of the chain are deprived, exploited, landless labourers who have no trade unions, no land and are kept under by military regimes – the depressed, marginalized, downtrodden poor. And their labour, exploited as it is, gives you and me cheaper food than we deserve. Is God pleased? I think God is angry. He is angry that the village of the world has produced the rich and luxurious and the poor – the exploited poor and starving.

Imagine a family living in a house: a happy family, good neighbours, popular people to meet, a happy Christian family. It is only after you have visited this family three or four times that you discover, living in the basement, three other families, living as slaves to the family above. Not seen, not mentioned, sometimes not known to be there; living with dripping walls, eating bread and water. And that rich, popular, happy family are Christians! It comes to the time of Lent and they say: 'What shall we do this Lent? We'll fast, shall we?' So they give up sugar in their tea. Then one of them says: 'What about those families down below . . . ought we to be doing something about them?' So they send some food down. But they still keep them as slaves. Then one of them says: 'What about releasing them?' But the others say: 'That's politics! The *status quo* is that we are rich and they are poor.' So they

have a happy Lent, giving up sugar in their tea; and have
a lovely Easter, during which the family below cooks for
them.

I am exaggerating. But am I exaggerating . . .? I do not
think so. This is the condition of the planet that God has
given us in which to spread the gospel of justice and peace,
love and mercy. Love does not mean just charitable giving
to people in prison. It means justice, liberation from prison.
Prisoners unjustly bound do not want kind and comforting
jailors, they want to be freed from prison. Christian love
is inevitably tied up with justice. Peace without justice is
no peace. Like that family living above the three slave
families, you and I are living on the rich fruits of our
exploited neighbours.

It is not only Mother Teresa who is the hero of modern
Christian living, with her wonderful charity to the poor in
Calcutta. There are also militant figures who see that
gospel living is not just charity to the oppressed but is
prophesying to the oppressors. In Archbishop Romero's
case that cost him his life, as it did for Jesus of Nazareth.

Prayer gives me the mind of Christ. It disturbs me
immensely. I ask myself: What can I do? Where can I go?
Who can I bind together with to do something about the
injustice of this world? And I am not immune to seeing
injustice in my own country . . . I am disturbed by seeing
the rich getting richer and the poor getting poorer. I am
disturbed that it may soon not be possible for people to
live in the country unless they have a motor car. This sort
of thing disturbs me . . . And I wonder whether I shouldn't
do something . . . Then a voice says: That's politics, not
Christianity! I open my New Testament, and the prophets
in the Old Testament, and I am immediately directed into
a bigger view of what the mind of Christ is and was. If
someone says, 'Remain neutral until you see all the facts

of the case,' I think of a statement by Edmund Burke: For evil to prosper it is simply sufficient for good people to do nothing. All this I find to be the disturbing fruit of prayer. The mind of Christ gives me much comfort when I am disturbed, but immense disturbance when I am too comfortable.

That brings me back again to the Christian Catholic parish. It should be a worshipping community and a pastoral caring community. It should also be an educating community, a formative community, an inspiring community, a prophetic, disturbing community. There should be much reading of the New Testament going on in parishes, and I am thankful we have several groups who open their New Testaments and let God disturb them. And they are all engaged in Third World Justice and Peace too, and with groups of handicapped people. You cannot have grace without mission. I think this element of the parish needs most developing in the future in our country. As the Old Testament prophets tell us, worship without justice stinks in the nostrils of God. Pastoral care is important, because where there is Christian care there must be love. but important also is formation, education, adult education, call it what you will. I want parishes to be vital centres of Christian dialogue, of thinking, disturbance, argument, brought almost to the brink of despair. The hope of the Spirit will keep us going.

This is where we can learn much from our non-Catholic Christian brethren, and join with them. In our parish, we have joint Bible study with our neighbouring congregations during Lent; and we are beginning to work together in justice projects, Third World projects, handicapped projects. I know it is important in the field of ecumenism for each Church to face each other and look at the differences and similarities. But I think it is particularly important at the parish level, because it is more feasible and more appropriate, that we should work together – not looking at each other across a table but walking side by side, looking at Christ's world. Brothers and sisters in the same Christ. We have to walk hand in hand, all Christians together. If you think I invented that phrase you are wrong! It was what the Pope said at Bellahouston: 'Let's walk hand in hand,' in life and work towards the Kingdom we are helping to build. Horizons . . .

Growth in the future must take place in two ways. Theologically, the diocese is the unit that matters in the Church; but sociologically, the parish is the most important unit. We know we belong to a parish. Parishes, especially in cities, have to grow down into smaller units, more or less temporary, more or less lasting. The large parish of 1,000-plus is marvellous for worship and care, but it is not an effective unit for gospel study and discipleship in Christ. In my parish we have forty-two base community sub-units, with two parish visitors each, with marvellous success. We have success; we have failure. We need to break down and let the Word of God speak in small groups so that, through grace, we can go out to mission. But we also have to develop the bigger unit of a diocesan consciousness – a consciousness of belonging not only to this parish, but to this diocese, because the bishop is, after all, the representative of Christ in the diocese.

What happens next? That is for you to decide. But at some point structures have to come in. You will need an ongoing, continuous diocesan pastoral structure. Parish, base community, diocese – all involve a sharing between priests and people. You will not be able to work together unless you allow yourselves to be broken. Priests must be broken from their clerical role, laity must be broken from their inherited attitudes of the past; then you can share.

After that will come the community of joy which is quite beyond words to express, but is deeply the will of Christ.

Appreciation*

During a light-hearted conversation recently, a few people were fantasizing – in that faintly absurd way we sometimes do – about the circumstances of their death. In his turn Father Jock said that, if he had a hand in arranging his own death, he would like to die while playing a round of golf with a friend!

It is not exactly the way you or I might have imagined the last moments of Jock Dalrymple. Discovered in the oratory on his knees in prayer, perhaps; visiting a parishioner in a cancer ward; or maybe sharing a bowl of soup with a crowd of 'down-and-outs' – but on the golf course?

Yet typical though our pictures may be, the circumstances of his death in America do reveal something of the character of the man, because he had gone to Florida to be with a friend, a missionary priest engaged in apostolic work in Latin America who was recuperating from illness. Still, I would like to know how the two men who have most disturbed my conscience about the oppressed of the Third World came to be playing golf in the heartland of

* This appreciation was a homily given by Father Charles Barclay at the Requiem Mass in St Ninian's, Edinburgh – the parish where Father Dalrymple had spent his last ten years. It stands practically unaltered.

middle America . . . There's surely a touch of divine comedy in that.

However we interpret the last days of Father Jock's life, we do know that the dominant theme of his life was his love for God, and 'that by turning everything to their good, God co-operates with those who love him'. Certainly, during these last ten years Jock felt that everything had 'come good'. As he himself said, his ten years in St Ninian's were the happiest and most contented of his life; and his death at this time seems almost right.

Father Jock had more than two years to prepare for that moment, since the first of his heart-attacks. Reflecting on his near-death, he realized afresh the old truth that, during life, each of us 'dies' over and over again. Each of these 'deaths' is surely painful. But they are also moments of liberation, for out of each 'death' God draws us on to new life in Christ, a more vigorous spiritual life, a more profound participation in the paschal mystery of our Lord's dying and rising. In this Mass, we proclaim the death of the Lord, and celebrate his resurrection. With confidence we pray that in Father Jock Dalrymple the glory of the risen Christ will now be fully revealed.

When you reflect on the Scriptures, as Jock did daily, you meet not only with inspiration and consolation, but also with a challenge: to enter more deeply into the rhythm of the suffering and a glorification of our Redeemer. The readings just proclaimed crystallise a challenge and a promise: be prepared to suffer and *thus* enter into glory.

Like any of us, Jock was afraid of suffering. His intuition warned him, and experience taught him, that interior suffering can be as intolerable as physical suffering, and he recoiled from it. Through time, with generosity of spirit and perseverance, he did yield to the invading, yet liberating force of God's grace; and to his delight and surprise discovered, as we can, how 'our present sufferings cannot be compared to the glory which is waiting for us'.

Jock poked fun at fashionable attention to the 'mid-life crisis'. Yet it was during his own middle years, roughly the years at Drygrange and Canmore and Muirhouse, that significant liberations happened in him.

By nature and education Jock Dalrypmple was rather conservative. But he surrendered his innate resistance to change when he responded to the teaching of the Church in the Vatican Council. His considerable intellect resonated to the major themes of the Council, especially those quarried from the Bible: the Church as sacrament of Jesus Christ, the embodiment of the risen Lord; and the Church as the pilgrim people of God. These took root in his heart, and twenty-five years on he could still thrill you with that vision. Mind you, he often had to screw his courage to the sticking-place to communicate his passion for the truth, as he saw it, for strong criticism was likely to follow; and from that too he wanted to shrink.

It was that same courage which helped him overcome the liabilities of his sometimes painful shyness and marked introversion of temperament. For he often found it difficult to communicate at the level of his emotions. He had a warm, even passionate, heart, but was inhibited in expressing his affection for people. In the boisterous, outgoing communities of seminary and university, it was painful to be timid in relationships, particularly if you looked a little austere, a bit forbidding, and were even regarded as somewhat aloof. Certainly, from school days on, he had always had a few close friends. But now the Lord prised open his heart, and a marvellous transformation took place, and he felt the freedom to enjoy an ever-expanding circle of friends.

We can thank God for redeeming our emotions, liberating our hearts to love. But the Lord desires to free us at every level, even the deepest. You know, for example, when you take seriously the call to 'be perfect as your heavenly Father is perfect', a curious twist occurs with the first fervour of conversion – it happened to Jock as well. We want to 'institutionalize' our spirituality; we want to domesticate and tame the Spirit of God, living by law rather than spirit. So we construct systems, invent rules, and settle for a religious externalism. It's the instinct within us to be in control of everything, including the Spirit of God.

From this too we have to be released. But at what cost! Many of the certainties which give security are lost to us, they die within us, and we die to them. More and more we are brought to rely ultimately on God alone. Jock's study of the great spiritual writers, John of the Cross above all, helped him to overcome his fear and risk the uncertainties.

But his surest ally in this process was not the mighty John of the Cross, but a young Carmelite nun, Thérèse of Lisieux. Her 'little way' of gospel simplicity inspired Jock to surrender the desire to be in control, and to let go, really believing that God 'has revealed these things to little children and concealed them from the learned and the clever'. It was not of course (it never is) a once-and-for-always event. It is a process which has to be repeated often, even daily, this surrender, this dying to fear that we might live more perfectly in love.

God, however, has chosen to redeem us, not as mere individuals, nor in isolation from one another. We belong to the human family and are called into a community of salvation.

Even more mystifying, God invites you and me to join with him as trusted collaborators in his great work of

148

liberating men and women from every kind of bondage – '. . . to share your bread with the hungry, and shelter the homeless poor, to clothe the one you see to be naked; to break unjust fetters, to let the oppressed go free'.

John Hamilton Dalrymple's share in the work of redemption was through the priesthood. It meant a kind of 'walking away' from his family, despite his great love for them; from a career; and from married life. For more than three decades he strove to minister to the flock of Christ, and through them and with them to care for a world desperately in need of Christ's liberating love. All his energies and talents, his limitations and weaknesses even, were placed at the disposal of this ministry of priesthood.

The conviction that the gospel opens up glorious possibilities for everyone compelled him to accept invitations here, there and everywhere to speak on Christian life. His prowess as a speaker and preacher paved the way for another apostolate, this time in the written word, and he spent himself unstintingly in both fields in his efforts to communicate Christ, crucified and risen from the dead.

Not only in word, but in action as well. While he was in the parish of St Mary's Cathedral, Edinburgh, with Greenside as his district, he developed an affection for the gospel's poor; those who live, as the Americans say, 'on the wrong side of the tracks'; the marginated, those deprived in any way whatsoever. It was this zeal which prompted the founding of Martin House – a foolhardy adventure if ever there was one – which for twenty years offered warm hospitality and realistic care for women in a variety of difficult situations.

It is not enough, the Lord tells us in the gospel, to offer shelter or bread or clothes: we are to offer our selves. For Father Jock this meant that his home – Marionville, Canmore, his room in Drygrange – was not only his, but

149

belonged to anyone who cared to avail themselves of his hospitality. How remarkable that this intensely private person should become virtually public property. I found myself, when looking forward to having Jock as a partner-in-ministry in Kirkcaldy, wondering rather ruefully how I would cope with having my home-life turned topsy-turvy. . .

But Father Jock had quite a way with him and, before you knew it, you were caught up in what he was doing. He would encourage and enable others to share with him in his enterprises. Members of the St Ninian's team ministry know this only too well. People in the parish also know this very well. The ministry to the poor became, in Jock's wry phrase, a ministry of the 'up-and-ins' to the 'down-and-outs' – and the mutual advantage of them both.

Jock's concern for the 'fourth world' at home was matched by his concern for the needs of our sisters and brothers in the 'third world'. With characteristic gusto, he threw himself into learning from the oppressed peoples of the southern hemisphere, and prompted discussion *and* action in the great issues of justice and peace throughout the world.

Father Jock spent twelve years in Drygrange. He contributed thoughtfully to the reshaping of seminary life, raised radical questions about the best ways of forming men for the priestly ministry. But it was as spiritual director that he made his greatest impact, particularly devoting his energies to developing a solid life of prayer in the priests of the future. In discussion, then as in later years, he delighted in tossing into the debate, provocative and sometimes outrageous statements, to startling effect when his listeners' opinions were shallow or ill-thought-out. To disconcerting effect, he employed, in personal counselling, the long, pregnant pause, which has become legendary among those of us who were with him as students. And he provoked much laughter when he would protest that his counselling was of the non-directive kind . . .

Even when he left Drygrange, many priests found in him a helpful and sure guide, a compassionate confessor, an understanding confidante. Though gentle, he did not compromise the radical demands of the gospel, urging us to rise above mediocrity, believing the dictum that 'the good is often the enemy of the best'.

As a priest, Father Jock always intended to point to Christ: 'He must increase, I must decrease.' More than any self-conscious advertizing for vocations, his manner of living the priesthood has helped make ordinations in this parish church an almost annual event.

Sinner that he knew himself to be, Jock threw himself on the mercy of God. 'This poor man called and the Lord heard him and rescued him.' The crucible of Father Jock's liberation was prayer. Despite his fluency in writing about prayer, his facility for teaching the ways of prayer, Jock did not always find praying easy, and perhaps only rarely so. Yes, he disciplined himself rigorously to prayer. But, like Jacob, he wrestled with God in long, lonely hours of prayer. Liberation came here when he ceased to struggle and wrestle, and was schooled to surrender himself to God. His prayer became less complex, as did his life, and more of a gentle and serene merging with God at the ground of his being. What wonders the Lord has worked in him. And, he would have us know, what wonders the Lord is working in our lives as well.

In a recent article Father Jock wrote:

When we have found our soul we can live fruitfully the ever-present tension caused by our high ideals received from the gospel and our distressingly low performance.

Appreciation

United in God in the depth of our being we can not only survive this tension but make it an instrument of our priestly work. At that deepest level God meets me and I meet God. At that level all is grace and sheer thanksgiving.

(*Clergy Review*, Sept. 1985)